ROADMAP™  B2

WORKBOOK
with key and online audio

Lindsay Warwick

CONTENTS

3

Vocabulary

Verbs with dependent prepositions

1 Match the sentence halves.

1 I don't believe ....
2 Does that car belong ....
3 Unfortunately, Richard suffers ....
4 Does the J in your name stand ....
5 I can't concentrate ....
6 Why are you smiling ....
7 I'm working ....
8 We have to deal ....

a to anyone you know?
b for James like your dad?
c in ghosts. Do you?
d on a really exciting project at the moment.
e on work when people are talking.
f from really bad headaches.
g with some really difficult customers at work.
h at me like that?

2 Complete the text with the words in the box and a preposition.

deal   relied   smile   stand   suffer   thinking   work

Running shy

I'm naturally a shy person so talking to people I don't know isn't easy. For a long time, I **¹** .... a few close friends for company. I didn't try to make new friends and I even chose a job where I didn't have to **²** .... strangers. In the end, I realised that I needed to make a change. I joined a running club where I could **³** .... improving both my confidence and my fitness. On my first day, I tried to make eye contact with everyone and **⁴** .... them. I even started a conversation. Slowly, I started to make friends. I'm now **⁵** .... starting my own running group for people who **⁶** .... social anxiety like me. I'd call it The RS Group. RS would **⁷** .... Running Shy.

Grammar

Question forms

3 Put the words in the correct order to make questions and sentences.

1 put / here / these books / who ?
   ....

2 the film / do you know / starts / what time ?
   ....

3 looking / you / are / at / who ?
   ....

4 any clubs / belong / you / to / do ?
   ....

5 how old / are / could I ask / you ?
   ....

6 why / here / wonder / yet / I / nobody's
   ....

7 this morning / who / you / called / so early ?
   ....

8 Tom / I'd love / gets / from / to know / his energy / where
   ....

4 Match the questions and sentences in Exercise 3 with answers a–h.

a You could, but I'm not sure I'll answer! ....
b Me too. He's always been really active. ....
c No one. Just watching everyone dance. ....
d I think it was Alex. They look like his. ....
e No. I'm a member of a gym but that's all. ....
f Maybe they're all stuck in traffic. ....
g Probably around eight. I'll look online. ....
h No idea. It was a wrong number. ....

5 Complete the prompts to make questions for the answers.

1 The shops usually close <u>at 6 p.m.</u>
   Can you tell me .... ?
2 BBC stands for <u>British Broadcasting Corporation</u>.
   What .... ?
3 <u>Dan</u> gave me this necklace.
   Who .... ?
4 Sam<u>'s probably shopping</u>.
   I wonder ....
5 We're working on <u>the Richbell project</u>.
   Which .... ?
6 Matt was rude to you yesterday because <u>you ignored him last week</u>.
   I'd really like to know ....
7 <u>Nothing happened</u> after the meal last night. We all left and went home.
   What .... ?
8 Anna's visited <u>a lot of countries</u>. Over 90!
   I'd love to know ....

Vocabulary

Phrases to describe emotions

1 Match phrases 1–8 with definitions a–h.

1 have a big impact on someone _____
2 be a total fool _____
3 feel numb _____
4 devastating _____
5 inspire someone to do something _____
6 blow your mind _____
7 be in shock _____
8 bawl your eyes out _____

a cry very hard
b affect someone a lot
c be very stupid
d be very surprised
e have no feeling
f extremely upsetting
g cause someone to do something
h impress/excite/astonish you very much

2 Complete the social media post with the phrases in the box.

> a total fool   bawled my eyes out   believe her luck
> big impact   blew my mind   feel ashamed   in shock
> inspired me

orge White   Yesterday at 20.21

...neone once told me that if ...mething is worth doing, it's ...rth doing well. That had a
_____
...me and it's something I've tried ...do ever since. So, with that in ...d, here's how I proposed to ... girlfriend Lizzie today.

...mments

onnie So romantic! I ² _____ when
...watched it. In fact, I've only just stopped crying.

...eon I'm ³ _____ . You planned all
...is and didn't tell me?! 😮

...lvaro I proposed to my partner in a supermarket and you did it
...e that? I ⁴ _____ that my effort was
...o poor.

...lax Congratulations! Amazing news and amazing proposal. You've
_____ to ask your sister to marry me
...ow. Do you think she'll say yes?!

Eve Why don't you ask me and find out?

George You'd be ⁶ _____ if
you didn't.

lara I'm so happy for you guys. I bet Lizzie couldn't
_____ when she saw that ring. Beautiful!

Lizzie I couldn't. The whole thing was a surprise and completely
⁸ _____ .

Grammar

Past simple, past continuous, *used to*, *would*, *keep* + *-ing*

3 Choose the correct alternatives.

1 While I *waited/was waiting* for the bus yesterday, I *saw/was seeing* an old friend from school.
2 Leo *used to/would* like steak but he doesn't anymore.
3 We were at the beach. The sun *used to come down/ was coming down* and it *would get/was getting* dark.
4 Sam stopped during the race but I *kept/was* going.
5 When we were little, we*'d go/were going* to the woods every day after school.
6 Barcelona *beat/beating* Real Madrid 1–0 yesterday.

4 Correct six mistakes with past verb forms.

I was a good student at school and the head teacher was often giving me extra responsibilities. One day, though, I was doing something really silly. My classmates and I were sitting in our classroom, were waiting for the teacher. One boy, Tom, realised that our next test paper was sitting in an envelope on the teacher's desk so we were deciding to take a really quick look. Of course, the teacher caught us and we got into trouble. The head teacher told me he couldn't give me any more responsibilities. I would feel very ashamed of myself at that moment. However, my dad said, 'You have to make the best out of a bad situation. Now you can concentrate on your studies.' I was never forgetting that piece of advice.

5 Make sentences in the past using the prompts.

1 While / I / sit / outside this morning / I / see / a really unusual looking bird.
_____
_____

2 Although / Maddie / take / loads of driving lessons last year, / she / fail / her test.
_____
_____

3 André / used / work at the local bank but now he / have / his own business.
_____
_____

4 We / look / at the menu / try / to decide what to eat.
_____
_____

5 My family and I / often / go / camping / in the summer holidays.
_____
_____

6 I / once / break / a finger / while / I /play / basketball.
_____

Vocabulary

Adjectives of character

1 Put the letters in order to make adjectives of character. The first letter is underlined.

1 g<u>t</u>uigno<u>o</u> ....
2 tsa<u>c</u>iuou ....
3 veders<u>r</u>e ....
4 tuvod<u>a</u>rensu ....
5 sutrgi<u>n</u>t ....
6 ed<u>o</u>girasn ....
7 f<u>c</u>dnentoi ....
8 cus<u>s</u>opisiu ....

2 Choose the correct alternatives.

1 My brother never takes risks. He's naturally a *cautious/confident* person.
2 I can be quite a *careless/nervous* driver. I don't always pay attention to other drivers.
3 Kim believes that everyone is good but personally, I think she's too *suspicious/trusting* of others.
4 I'd love to be *adventurous/organised* like my cousin and travel to unusual places all over the world.
5 Paul seems happy but he's *nervous/reserved* so doesn't show his feelings much.
6 People say that I'm *adventurous/outgoing* because I love talking to people but I used to be quite shy.
7 I'm quite a *careless/suspicious* person. I don't trust others easily and don't believe they're all good.
8 My colleague Fran is so *cautious/organised*. She plans everything really carefully.

Language focus

Verb + noun collocations

3 Match the sentence halves.

1 I don't mind waiting ....
2 We should all make ....
3 If you think you're going to lose ....
4 It's good to take ....
5 It's good to speak ....
6 I'm not very good at meeting ....

a in line. I use the time to check my messages.
b deadlines. I'm often late with my work.
c your temper, count to ten.
d your mind at work if you do it politely.
e more time for fun with our friends.
f an interest in your friends' lives.

4 Choose the correct option a, b or c.

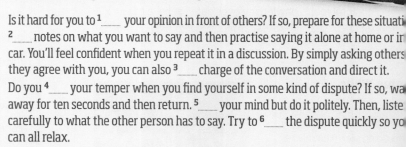

Changing your character

Fed up with some of your character traits? Feel like a change? Here are some tips.

Is it hard for you to **1** .... your opinion in front of others? If so, prepare for these situati[...] **2** .... notes on what you want to say and then practise saying it alone at home or in[...] car. You'll feel confident when you repeat it in a discussion. By simply asking others[...] they agree with you, you can also **3** .... charge of the conversation and direct it.
Do you **4** .... your temper when you find yourself in some kind of dispute? If so, wa[...] away for ten seconds and then return. **5** .... your mind but do it politely. Then, liste[...] carefully to what the other person has to say. Try to **6** .... the dispute quickly so yo[...] can all relax.

1	a	say	b	tell	c voice
2	a	Take	b	Do	c Get
3	a	have	b	take	c make
4	a	give	b	have	c lose
5	a	Speak	b	Say	c Talk
6	a	resolve	b	work	c decide

5 Rewrite the sentences using the words in bold so they mean the same.

1 It's not possible to understand this article. **MAKE/SENSE**
....

2 You'll have to join a row of people to get the tickets. **WAIT/LINE**
....

3 None of my colleagues are curious about my work. **TAKE/INTEREST**
....

4 If we don't finish our work by a specific time, we'll be in trouble. **MEET/DEADLINE**
....

5 If you feed our cat while we're away, I'll do it for you when you next go away. **RETURN/FAVOUR**
....

Vocabulary
Verbs to describe a healthy lifestyle

1 Choose the correct option a, b or c.

An expensive watch

Last year, I decided to invest in a watch that
¹_____ my fitness levels. It ²_____ information
about how far I run or walk when I do
exercise and ³_____ me to try to go faster
each time. It also records the number of
steps I do and reminds me to get up and
walk around every hour when I'm at work.
All in all, it ⁴_____ a much healthier lifestyle
and ⁵_____ it possible for me to get fitter.
This all sounds great, doesn't it? And it was
at first – I loved it! But it wasn't long before
that changed. After a few months, while
I was still noting how many steps I was
doing, I was doing nothing to increase the
number. The reminders that ⁶_____ me
from being lazy went ignored. I even
stopped recording my running times.
Now, it's basically nothing more than an
expensive watch!

1 a warns
   b encourages
   c tracks
2 a provides
   b discourages
   c makes
3 a offers
   b encourages
   c warns
4 a makes
   b provides
   c promotes
5 a did
   b got
   c made
6 a warned
   b discouraged
   c avoided

English in action
Contribute effectively to a conversation or discussion

2 Put the words in the correct order to make sentences and questions.

1 makes / say / what / that / you ?

2 really / not / on / I'm / that one / you / with

3 a bit / you / more / can / that / explain ?

4 guess / right, / you / I / be / might

5 me / happened / once / that / to

6 you / that conclusion / to / how / come / did ?

7 way / you / it / could / look at / another

8 of / reminds / the time / that / to Spain / me / I went

3 Complete the conversations with phrases using the words in brackets.

1 **A:** Fitness gadgets are only helpful if you make an effort to get fit.
   B: _____ (absolutely/right). There's no
   point having one if you don't.
2 **A:** Chocolate's good for you? _____
   (make/say)?
   B: Well, experts say a little of the dark variety can be good for your heart.
3 **A:** Parents should get a fine if they give their children unhealthy food.
   B: _____ (serious)? That's a crazy idea!
4 **A:** The key to good physical health is to eat less and move more!
   B: _____ (got/point) but that's easier to say
   than do.
5 **A:** The price of sweets should be higher. It'll stop people from eating them.
   B: _____ (experience), that kind of tax
   doesn't work. People just spend more.
6 **A:** Education leads to a healthy diet? _____
   (come/conclusion)?
   B: Research. When we know what healthy food is, we eat better.

4 Complete the blog post with a suitable word.

'If you want to get fit you've got a few ¹_____ . One is to join a gym.
The ²_____ advantage of that is that you have access to lots of
different equipment as well as maybe a pool. The ³_____ is that it can
be expensive, particularly if you don't go very often. Another argument
⁴_____ the gym is that it's a routine which can get very boring very
quickly. Another ⁵_____ , however, is to walk or run. The ⁶_____
of this is that it's free and you can get outside and see some great views
at the same time. You have to take into ⁷_____ that the air might not
be very clean if you live in a city, though.
On ⁸_____ , I think that walking or running is preferable to joining
a gym because it's a more natural form of exercise than lifting weights.
However, everyone will have their own preference.'

Reading

1 Read the heading and introduction in the text. What kind of text do you think it is? Read the whole text and check your answer.

1 Descriptive article

2 Opinion essay

3 Research report

2 Read the article again and choose the correct option a, b or c.

1 Sophie set up a blind date because _____
  a her friend suggested it.
  b her married friends met that way.
  c she rarely meets new people.

2 Before her date, Sophie knew _____
  a a lot about her date.
  b a little about her date.
  c nothing about her date.

3 What was different about Sophie's evening out? _____
  a She spent more time on her appearance than usual.
  b It was her first time at the Italian restaurant.
  c She felt uncommonly nervous about the situation.

4 Why do you think Lucas said he could tell that Sophie was a journalist? _____
  a She was more talkative than he was.
  b She asked him a lot of questions.
  c She chatted a lot about her work.

5 What does Sophie say is the advantage of a traditional blind date? _____
  a You get to learn about the person directly from them.
  b You can share your experiences with friends online.
  c You don't have to spend a lot of time with the person.

6 What might Sophie say about her experience? _____
  a 'It's something all my friends have tried at one time or another.'
  b 'There are only benefits to traditional dating.'
  c 'I'm glad I tried it but I doubt I'll do it again.'

3 Choose the correct alternatives.

1 In the introduction, 'which' in the final line refers back to *traditional offline dating is dead/ half my married friends met their partners online*.

2 In paragraph 3, Sophie says she took 'far longer to get ready' which means she took *less time/ much more time*.

3 In paragraph 6, Sophie starts by asking a question to *introduce a new topic/ get answers from the reader*.

4 Find the phrases in the box in the article. Then, match them with definitions 1–8.

be relieved
converse with
fall into easy conversation
hit it off (with someone)
make a positive impression
make judgements (about someone)
put someone at ease
tell (something)

1 know something because of certain signs that show it
_____

2 talk to (more formal)
_____

3 begin to talk comfortably
_____

4 get on well
_____

5 form opinions
_____

6 encourage someone to have a good feeling about you
_____

7 make someone feel relaxed
_____

8 feel happy because you stop worrying about something
_____

5 Complete the forum posts with some of the phrases in Exercise 4.

Sara Today 09.26

It's interesting that you enjoyed not knowing anything about Lucas. We always want to make a positive ¹_____ which means we often present only our best selves online. Even when we hit it ²_____ with someone online and fall into an ³_____ , we control what we say more than we do face-to-face. We can't really ⁴_____ what kind of person they are.

Richard Today 10.03

I agree with Sara to a point. However, it's so much easier to converse ⁵_____ new people online than face-to-face these days, and we ⁶_____ judgements about people in the real world, too.

Dating in an offline world

By Sophie Black

Most of my married friends met their partners online. They developed their relationships via the internet rather than go to the cinema or to a restaurant as people did in the past. It seems as if traditional offline dating is dead, which is why I decided to give it a go.

[1]I'm a pretty reserved person so don't have much luck making friends, either online or in the real world. I don't belong to any clubs and I mostly work from home, so the only person I converse with regularly is my 65-year-old postman. I was fed up of being single so one day I gathered some courage and asked my friend Josie to set me up on a blind date. She thought I was mad but, after some persuasion, agreed.

[2]For those of you who aren't familiar with traditional dating, a blind date is one where you don't know each other. It's usually organised by a friend who thinks you'll hit it off. All I knew about my date was that his name was Lucas, he was Josie's colleague and he was a couple of years older than me.

[3]On the day of the date, it took me far longer to get ready than normal. I wanted to be sure that I looked my best and made a positive first impression. I also wanted to be in a familiar setting to put me at ease so I suggested that we meet at an Italian restaurant not far from where I live. It's an old favourite – somewhere nice but not too formal.

[4]By the time I got to the restaurant, my heart was thumping in my chest and I couldn't quite catch my breath. So much for being at ease. It wasn't unusual for me to feel this way but I wanted to avoid a full-blown panic attack, so I forced myself to take some deep breaths to calm down. It seemed to work, which was just as well because right at that moment, Lucas walked in. He turned and smiled at me. I felt immediately relieved.

[5]We sat down and fell into easy conversation where we both chatted a lot. He showed an interest in my work and I asked him a lot about his job and his family. He told me that he could tell I was a journalist! At the end of the evening, we swapped mobile numbers and agreed to keep in touch.

[6]So, how was the experience? Well, like anything, there were pros and cons. The main benefit for me was the fact that we knew nothing about each other at the start of the date. These days, we usually make judgements about a person before we meet them based on their social media profile. It was great to get to know the real Lucas and not the one he portrays online.

[7]On the other hand, two hours is a long time to spend with someone in awkward silence. It wasn't the case with Lucas, but it could be with someone else, and that's a downside for me. You can't just walk off in the way you can switch off your phone when a conversation isn't going your way.

[8]Will I stick with traditional dating? Possibly. It was an enjoyable experience – and, despite its drawbacks, one I'd certainly recommend to friends who limit themselves to online dating. However, as it's not the normal way to meet people any more, probably not. I think I'll just have to make more of an effort online or join a club.

Listening

1 🔊 **1.01 Listen to the first part of a radio interview. What is the topic?**

  a How to identify a person's character

  b How negative characteristics can be positive

  c How we develop certain characteristics

2 🔊 **1.02 Listen to the full interview. Match each characteristic in the box with its definition.**

> boredom laziness messiness optimism
> pessimism shyness

  1 the regular belief that good things will happen

  2 the regular belief that bad things will happen

  3 not liking work or physical activity

  4 the feeling of being nervous about meeting people

  5 being untidy

  6 the feeling you get when nothing is interesting

3 **Listen again. Match characteristics 1–6 with descriptions a–f.**

  1 laziness

  2 messiness

  3 boredom

  4 optimism

  5 pessimism

  6 shyness

  a Takes more care of himself

  b Looks for new activities or information

  c Makes a good leader

  d Makes or designs new ways of doing things

  e Doesn't prepare for bad situations

  f More willing to do things that could go wrong

4 **Complete the summary with the words in the box. Then listen and check.**

> attention creative inventions leaders
> prepare risks

We think of negative characters as bad but actually they can be positive. Laziness can result in new **1**＿＿＿＿ because lazy people want to make life less difficult. Messiness is a sign of creativity. Messy people also take more **2**＿＿＿＿ . Bored people search for new activities or knowledge and become more **3**＿＿＿＿ . Pessimistic people **4**＿＿＿＿ for bad things happening and so they actually live safer lives. Finally, shy people listen carefully and pay more **5**＿＿＿＿ to what's happening around them. Shy people can be very good **6**＿＿＿＿ .

Writing

1 **Read the description and choose the best title.**

  1 A place I know well

  2 A place that disappointed me

  3 A place that surprised me

  4 A place I'd like to visit

a<u>I love it when I go somewhere that completely blows my mind.</u> It's not usually anywhere familiar from TV. It's usually the places that I have no expectations of. Last year, I visited the Summer Palace in Beijing. I got there early because I knew there'd be lots of visitors and I don't enjoy being in crowds. Even at 8.30 a.m., the entrance was full of people and **b**<u>I started to panic.</u> **c**<u>I felt like I was at a football match or a concert at one point, but then I arrived at the lake and felt a sense of openness which helped.</u> The lake was beautiful. It was bigger than I had imagined and **d**<u>sunlight was shimmering across it</u>. **e**<u>I could feel it on the back of my neck, too.</u> It felt warm and lovely. I walked towards a park on the west side of the lake and found a quiet place to sit down. There, I spent an hour just watching **f**<u>excited people surround the elegant palace buildings</u>. I could hear the gentle waves of the water hitting the side of the lake as boats went past. It was so peaceful. **g**<u>Not something I'd expected.</u>

2 **Read the description again. Are the sentences true (T) or false (F)?**

1 The writer thinks that well-known places are often surprising. ....

2 The writer arrived early to make the most of the day. ....

3 The writer doesn't like being in large crowds. ....

4 The weather was good. ....

5 The size of the lake was as expected. ....

6 The writer found a peaceful place to enjoy. ....

3 **Read the Focus box. Then, match examples a–g in the description with 1–7 in the box.**

Adding interest to a description

1 Start by mentioning the theme of the description. ....

2 Describe what you can see but also describe what you can smell, hear and feel. ....

3 Describe action or movement. What were the people doing? What were the animals or insects doing? What were the trees and clouds doing? ....

4 Describe your reaction to the place. How did it make you feel? ....

5 Compare things to other things using *like*, for example, compare how you felt or what something looked like. ....

6 Use interesting verbs and adjectives to describe these things. ....

7 Come back to the theme at the end. ....

4 **Complete the description with phrases and sentences a–f.**

¹........ . Last autumn, my friend persuaded me to take a beach holiday to Thailand with her. I wasn't all that excited and so I let her choose the hotel. I was expecting the usual family hotel with pool but she surprised me with a very exclusive resort. As soon as I walked into the hotel lobby, I knew it was special. The floor was white with gold patterns. It was so shiny, ²........ . The ceiling was high with large fans keeping us cool. ³........ . There were white sofas to our right, divided by large, ⁴........ plants. Smartly-dressed guests were sitting there chatting. The staff all wore ⁵........ uniforms without a patch of dirt on them. They smiled politely at us as they walked past. Out of the window, I could see the sea. It was a gorgeous blue. ⁶........ .

a bright white

b I could feel the light breeze on my face.

c It's always lovely when a place surprises you.

d it was almost like a mirror

e I was in shock at the beauty around me, but it was a very welcome surprise

f beautiful-smelling

5 **Read the description in Exercise 4 again. What does the writer compare to a mirror? What word do they use to make this comparison?**

6 **Match sentences 1–4 with a–d to make comparisons.**

1 There I was, alone in the middle of the desert. ....

2 Suddenly, it started pouring with rain. ....

3 The kitchen was warm and inviting. ....

4 The room was filled with antiques and golden furniture. ....

a It smelt like coffee and burnt toast.

b It looked like a museum.

c It sounded like hundreds of people drumming on the roof.

d It felt like I was the only person in the world.

7 **Complete the comparisons with your own ideas.**

1 The snow crunched beneath our feet. It felt like …

2 Waves crashed against the wall. It sounded like …

3 I took a deep breath. The market smelt like …

4 The field was covered in tents. It looked like …

Prepare

8 **You're going to write a description with the title *A place that surprised me*. Make notes about:**

- where the place was and what you expected
- why it surprised you
- what you could see, hear and smell
- how you felt
- what people were doing

9 **Organise your notes in Exercise 8 into a plan. Use the descriptions in Exercises 1 and 4, and the ideas in the Focus box to help you.**

Write

10 **Write your description. Use your plan in Exercise 9 to help you.**

11 **Edit your description. Use the following questions to help you:**

- Is there a clear theme?
- Have you used interesting verbs and adjectives?
- Have you made interesting comparisons?

2A

Vocabulary
Phrases with *get*

1 Choose the correct alternatives.

1 You look tired. You should get some *relaxation/rest*.
2 My room's full of stuff. I need to get *away with/rid of* it.
3 Is that the waiter? Can you try and get his *attention/awareness* for me, please?
4 Jack's so annoying. He really gets on my *bones/nerves*.
5 Sammy and I are getting *apart/together* on Monday.
6 I've got no money until I get *paid/salaried* on Friday.
7 Just get *immediate/straight* to the point and tell me what you want.
8 Was that a joke? Sorry, I didn't get *it/what*.

2 Complete the conversations with phrases using the correct form of *get* and the words in brackets.

1 A: Have you got Mark's number?
   B: Why? Do you need to _____ (touch) him?
2 A: Stop screaming at the TV. They can't hear you!
   B: I know but I always _____ (carried) when I watch rugby.
3 A: I'm off to Madrid for work tomorrow.
   B: Lucky you! I hope you _____ (see) some of the sights while you're there.
4 A: Do you ever _____ (feeling) that Mandy doesn't like us?
   B: Yes, she's always giving us evil looks.
5 A: Stop making that noise. It's _____ (nerves)!
   B: I know. That's why I'm doing it!
6 A: Do you want this old T-shirt or shall I _____ (rid) it?
   B: Don't throw it away! It's got sentimental value.
7 A: Tom's over there if you want to speak to him.
   B: Oh yeah. Can you wave at him and _____ (attention)?
8 A: I'm going to go to bed to _____ (rest) while Lily's asleep.
   B: Good idea. No doubt she'll want feeding again in an hour.

Grammar
Present perfect simple and continuous

3 Choose the correct endings.

1 I've been cleaning the house _____
   a all day today.   b for two hours yesterday.
2 Our English teacher has set us homework _____
   a three times this week.   b for weeks.
3 We've already _____
   a been having breakfast.   b had breakfast.
4 Ruth's been _____
   a enjoying her dance lessons lately.
   b liking her dance lessons last week.
5 I've finally thought of _____
   a you all day.   b a solution to the problem.
6 How long has Ali _____
   a learnt Spanish?   b been learning Spanish?
7 Have you _____
   a finished the report yet?   b been finishing the report yet?
8 You're covered in dirt. Have you _____
   a worked in the garden?   b been working in the garden?

4 Complete the text with the correct form of the verbs in brackets.

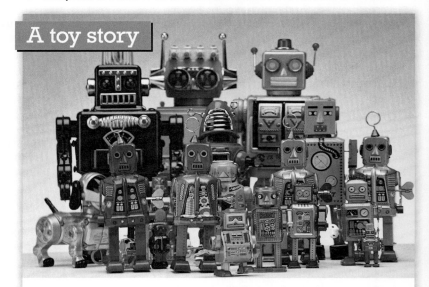

A toy story

When we think of social media influencers, we tend to think of young, trendy adults who talk about food, fashion and travel but this isn't necessarily true. Ryan **1** _____ (upload) videos of himself playing with toys since he was just four years old. Since then – 2015 – he **2** _____ (upload) a new video almost every day and **3** _____ (become) one of the most influential people on YouTube. Millions of children and adults **4** _____ (see) his videos and his channel **5** _____ (gain) over 18 million followers. According to Forbes, he **6** _____ (earn) over $22m. They even claimed he was the highest paid YouTuber in 2018. Of course, he doesn't do it on his own. His parents **7** _____ (support) him since the very beginning and continue to do so today.

Vocabulary

Social action

1 Complete the crossword with a noun that follows verbs 1–6.

Across
1 take (6)
3 enforce (1, 3)
5 increase (7)
6 carry out (8)

Down
2 warn about (3, 7)
3 tackle (1, 7)
4 offer (12)

2 Complete the news story with the correct verbs.

The education minister Nick Stanton has rejected a call to **¹b**_____ mobile phones in the classroom, saying that such a law would be hard to **²e**_____ . He also stated that individual head teachers should be able to decide whether or not to **³c**_____ down on mobile phone use. Research **⁴c**_____ out by the government reports that half of teens are almost always online and politicians have called for schools to **⁵d**_____ more to prevent the use of mobile phones in class. Mr Stanton says that schools should **⁶w**_____ teenagers about the dangers of too much screen time, but also teach them how best to use technology for learning.

Janet Smith, leader of the Teachers' Union, has said that schools can only **⁷t**_____ these problems if the government **⁸i**_____ school funding.

3 Rewrite the underlined words with phrases using the words in brackets.

1 Ministers say teens are online too much and it's time for schools to <u>do something about it</u>.   (action)
2 Parents say that schools should <u>provide other choices</u> to using mobile phones in lessons.   (offer)
3 Some teachers say that it's not their responsibility to <u>deal with the issue</u>.   (problem)
4 They say parents should <u>make</u> their children <u>aware of the harm</u> of too much screen time.   (warn)
5 Not all schools would be happy to <u>make sure a rule is obeyed</u> that bans mobile phones in schools.   (law)
6 Most people agree that we need to <u>increase the number of actions</u> to teach young people about using technology sensibly.   (more)

Grammar

The passive

4 Choose the correct alternatives.

1 Lots of new houses are *built/ being built* around here at the moment.
2 The town hall *hit/ was hit* by lightning last night.
3 We all ate the food that *had been/ be* prepared for us.
4 All the staff should *be given/ given* a share of the profits.
5 You must *get/ be got* a ticket before the day of the concert.
6 Fill in the form and you'll be *send/ sent* a free copy of the book.
7 My friends and I *speak/ are spoken* eight languages between us.
8 The salary was really bad so none of us wanted to *be given/ give* the job.

5 Complete the text with the correct active or passive form of the verbs in the box.

| get | give (x3) | invite | organise | also/offer | receive |
| start | train | | | | |

Young people from difficult backgrounds **¹**_____ the opportunity to learn to skateboard by a skateboarding charity. Each year, the Harold Hunter Foundation **²**_____ a range of skateboarding activities for young people. The charity, which **³**_____ in 2006, aims to help children and teens stick to positive activities in their lives. For well over a decade, youths in New York **⁴**_____ to attend clinics where they **⁵**_____ in skateboarding skills by adult instructors. Summer camp places **⁶**_____ . So far, 185 scholarships **⁷**_____ to skateboarders who **⁸**_____ both funding and equipment and it's hoped that more will **⁹**_____ the opportunity to do so in the future. Campers can attend three camps over three summers to build long-term relationships. The charity believes that the skills and confidence young people **¹⁰**_____ through skateboarding will help them to achieve success in life.

Skateboarding to success

2c

Vocabulary
Common complaints

1 Match the phrases in the box with situations 1–8.

> aggressive salesperson billing dispute
> broken promise cold caller false advertising
> faulty product lack of communication slow delivery

1 Someone tries to sell you new windows over the phone.
2 A pair of speakers that you bought don't work.
3 Your takeout order takes longer to arrive than expected.
4 Someone tries to sell you insurance in a slightly scary way.
5 Your new car uses far more fuel than the manufacturer said it would.
6 You disagree with an online shop about the amount you paid for some clothes.
7 A supermarket fails to give you information about your food shopping delivery.
8 Your mobile phone company says they'll replace your broken phone but they don't.

2 Choose the correct option a, b or c.

Avoiding problems when shopping online

Shopping online might be convenient but there are always issues to deal with. Companies are only legally obliged to return payment for ¹_____ products although many large companies do so for all returns. This is good because while the product may look fantastic in the photo, it can be somewhat disappointing in real life. While this is annoying, it isn't exactly ²_____ advertising so you can't legally ask for your money back. It's important to check for hidden costs to avoid billing ³_____. Extra delivery costs are a good example. ⁴_____ delivery might mean the product arrives after you need it so always check delivery times. Call a company to confirm the delivery date before you book the day off work. You may find the date has changed but ⁵_____ customer service means they've forgotten to tell you. You don't want to waste a day's holiday because of a ⁶_____ of communication and a ⁷_____ promise. Hopefully you'll find the customer service department is full of helpful, not rude, ⁸_____.

	a		b		c
1	empty		broken		faulty
2	false		wrong		incorrect
3	arguments		disputes		rows
4	Slow		Long		Short
5	weak		poor		ill
6	reduction		drop		lack
7	damaged		harmful		broken
8	staff		profession		labour

Language focus
-ed and -ing adjectives

3 Correct the mistakes in five of the sentences.

1 It's really frustrated when you burn a meal.
2 Running makes me so exhausted that I can only do it at the weekends.
3 I found that lecture really inspired.
4 Am I the only one that's alarming by what Jack just said?
5 I'm not convincing that we're going to get this project finished on time.
6 That last piece of cake is tempted but I've had enough.

4 Complete the pairs of sentences with the correct endings A or B.

1 We never watch the news these days. It's just too _____
2 It's not a good idea to watch the news if you're already _____
   A depressing   B depressed

3 Andy always interrupts me. It's _____
4 Someone just pushed into the queue and got the last ticket. I'm _____
   A infuriated!   B infuriating!

5 I'm 49 but have just been given a ticket for over 60s. I feel quite _____
6 My boss has asked us to work extra for no more pay. It's _____
   A insulting!   B insulted!

5 Complete the conversations with the correct form of the adjectives in the box.

> astonish confuse entertain exhaust satisfy
> tempt

1 A: Is it just me or is this information _____?
   B: It's not just you. I don't get it either.
2 A: I love it when I do everything on my 'to do' list.
   B: Oh, I know. It's really _____, isn't it?
3 A: I'm _____ that Max and Mel are a couple.
   B: I know. I was really surprised, too.
4 A: I'm _____ to try that pumpkin ice cream.
   B: Really? It sounds disgusting!
5 A: This isn't the most intelligent film I've ever seen.
   B: No, but it's _____ so that's OK.
6 A: It's been a long day. I'm _____.
   B: Yes, an early night for both of us, I think.

2

Listening

1 🔊 **2.01 Listen to a podcast. What's Marco's main point?**

  a Complaining can help you feel better in the long term.

  b The best way to complain is to tell other people your feelings.

  c We should try to change negative thoughts into positive thoughts.

2 Listen again. Complete the notes with one or two words in each gap.

Alicia's colleague complains about temperature, lateness and ¹ _____ .

Marco says that complaining doesn't improve ² _____ for long.

In one study, 50 percent of participants wrote about negative things that ³ _____ them.

The participants focusing on negative things were not as ⁴ _____ as those focusing on the positive.

Complaining can lead to stress which can cause ⁵ _____ to rise.

Complaining can affect how the ⁶ _____ feels, too.

It's a good idea to listen to a complainer and ⁷ _____ .

Asking the person how they'll improve the ⁸ _____ is also useful.

People write about things they're ⁹ _____ for in a gratitude diary.

Alicia appreciated her colleague's humour, help and ¹⁰ _____ !

3 Complete the sentences with the words in the box. Then, listen again and check.

> content   down   focus   frustrations   made up
> mindset   moan   negativity

  1 What didn't she _____ about? The temperature of the office for one.

  2 She complained if someone was late, even if they _____ the hours at the end of the day.

  3 Complaining helps to get out your _____ .

  4 Complaining produces feelings of _____ .

  5 The complainer brings the listener _____ .

  6 That might _____ their attention on finding a solution.

  7 It can help to change your _____ , or so people claim.

  8 Then, you'll both be _____ .

4 Match the words and phrases in the box with meanings 1–8.

> bring someone down   change your mindset   content
> focus your attention on   frustrations   make up
> moan   negativity

  1 work extra hours because you didn't do as much as you should have before _____

  2 reduce someone's happiness level _____

  3 feelings of being annoyed _____

  4 think about one thing very carefully _____

  5 to complain _____

  6 happy and satisfied _____

  7 attitude where you think of only bad things about someone/something _____

  8 make your general attitude/way of thinking different _____

5 🔊 **2.02 Read the sentences and choose the word you think the speaker will say next. Then, listen and check your answers.**

  1 I know your boss can be really tough on you but don't let him bring you _____ .

  2 Stop being so negative all the time. Be more positive and change your _____ .

  3 I go home and moan about work for five minutes every day. It helps me to get rid of all my _____ .

  4 Sorry I'm late – I promise I'll make the time _____ .

  5 It doesn't take much to make me happy. A hot bath, relaxing music and I'm _____ .

  6 You're such a complainer. All you do is _____ !

  7 I'm so tired. I can't seem to _____ on my work.

  8 There's a lot of _____ in here today. Why is everyone so miserable?

Reading

1 Read the title and introduction in the article. What is the main purpose of the article?

a   To highlight the dangers of gamification in the real world

b   To justify why gamification should be limited to entertainment

c   To outline the early stages of wider experimenting with gamification

2 In which paragraphs can you find the following information?

1   An example of gamification designed to create more profits   ....

2   Examples of what motivates people to play games   ....

3   Reasons why gamification might not work (two paragraphs)   ....

4   A definition of gamification   ....

5   An example of ineffective use of gamification   ....

6   An evaluation of studies into gamification   ....

7   A list of industries where gamification is being used   ....

8   An example of gamification used to cause social change   ....

3 Complete the sentences with words in the article.

1   Games reward players when they ....

2   Governments use gamification to encourage people to
....

3   In Sweden, motorists who drove ....
were given the chance to win money.

4   A system set up by a sports company rewarded the amount of
.... used daily.

5   This reward system encourages customers to stay
.... to the company.

6   In one company, employees got points when they responded to
.... on a company noticeboard.

7   Gamification is being used in the health industry, design and
....

8   The writer suggests that people who don't
.... a gamified system will not feel motivated.

9   Gamification will only work if game mechanics are
.... to a situation.

10 Leader boards don't work when players focus on the people
....

4 Match definitions 1–10 with words and phrases in the article.

1   idea (introduction)   ....

2   appearing (paragraph 1)   ....

3   health and happiness (paragraph 2)   ....

4   without any pattern (paragraph 2)   ....

5   help sell a product (paragraph 3)   ....

6   a situation which ends well for everyone (paragraph 3)   ....

7   changed (paragraph 3)   ....

8   stop people from feeling motivated (paragraph 4)   ....

9   doesn't achieve what it's expected to achieve (paragraph 5)   ....

10 situation (paragraph 6)   ....

5 Complete the sentences with the correct form of the words and phrases in Exercise 4.

1   Gaming can have a negative effect on the player's physical ....

2   Many of the skills learnt online can be applied to real-world ....

3   It's a .... The company gets free advertising and we get a free game.

4   It had the opposite effect – he was .... and didn't want to continue.

5   Sadly, the game proved .... when trialled with real patients.

6   The YouTube star was paid $1 million to help .... the game online.

7   It doesn't make sense. The game seems to reward players ....!

8   The company believes gamification will .... the workplace.

9   New apps seem to .... every other day.

10 Using gamification elements in this way is not a new ....

6 Which of these statements do you think the writer is likely to agree with?

1   Gamification mechanics can be applied in the same way everywhere.

2   Gamification can work if it's used properly.

3   When we get more research, we'll know more about what gamification works and what doesn't.

4   Gamification in education can't work.

5   Gamification should encourage people to focus on their own performance, not the performance of others.

6   It's easy for companies to apply gamification techniques to their advertising campaigns.

Gamification is a concept which is no longer seen only in video games and apps. It's now something that companies and governments are beginning to use to persuade people to behave in certain ways. Evan Young takes a look at what exactly it is and how it's being used.

[1] Video games are hugely popular these days. Not just amongst children, but more significantly amongst adults. Games encourage us to play by engaging us, making the next level challenging but achievable and giving us rewards when we perform successfully. It's these game mechanics that non-game organisations and governments are using to try to encourage people to change their behaviour. Gamification, as it's called, is popping up all over the place.

[2] Governments concerned with citizens' well-being are using gamification to persuade people to behave more positively. One example in Sweden was aimed at reducing drivers' road speed. Rather than only fine drivers when they went over the speed limit, they also entered drivers into a lottery each time they drove under the speed limit. Each month, one lucky driver's name was picked at random and they received the money that speeding drivers paid in fines.

[3] Companies are also using gamification to promote their brands and their products, as well as motivate employees to perform well. One sports company encourages customers to download an app and compete against each other to use the most physical energy each day. In doing so, they get rewards and remain loyal to the brand. It's a win-win for everyone. One global business consultancy company wanted their staff to communicate more effectively with each other and with their customers. To encourage this, the company set up a points system where staff members receive points for sharing information about company activities on their social media page, publishing a blog post on the company website and posting or replying to posts on their internal communication pages. Points are transformed into rewards.

[4] Gamification is also being used in education, design and the health industry, but does it actually work? Research carried out so far suggests that, while it can have a positive effect on motivation, gamification is in its infancy. Much more research is needed to truly know whether its impact is entirely positive or whether it can demotivate people who don't fully support the idea. After all, if you don't buy into the idea, you're less likely to participate but might feel irritated when colleagues do participate and are rewarded.

[5] What experts do say is that the success of gamification depends on how effectively game mechanics are applied to the situation. In schools, for example, games in class have shown in studies that students spend more time learning with games than without them, by choice. However, the learning isn't necessarily more effective than learning without a game. Why not? Because the game mechanics were ineffective. For example, students paid too much attention to what was happening at the top of the leader board and not enough on their own score. By giving students more information about their own performance, they can focus much more on making progress themselves.

[6] Of course, what works well in one situation may not work well in another. So, it's also a case of applying game mechanics in the best way for your context.

Writing

1 Read the email from Danny. Is he giving you good news, bad news or both?

2 Read the email again and answer the questions.

1 Why has Danny taken so long to reply?

2 What is Danny's good news?

3 Why is he always so tired at the weekend?

4 What are the advantages of Danny's job?

5 Why wasn't Danny able to buy the house he wanted?

6 What is he looking for now?

3 Read the email again. What's the purpose of phrases 1–3, asking for news or giving news?

4 Put the words in the correct order to make sentences. Then, match them with the headings in the box.

Asking for news   Giving news   Reacting to good news
Reacting to bad news

1 really / hear / I'm / about / sorry / to / your aunt

2 news / your / about / job / great

3 going / at work / it / How's ?

4 pleased / I'm / about / your exam results / hear / to / really

5 heard / you / Kate / about / have ?

6 recently / doing / you / been / have / what ?

7 me, / taken up / for / I've / as / a new hobby

8 so / your cat / sorry / I'm / about

18 March

Hi!

Sorry I've not been in touch for a while. ¹I've been really busy with work recently and I just haven't had time for much else.

²I finally got that promotion I wanted last month. I was really pleased when it was finally announced, but it means that I'm working on some really big projects that require a lot of attention. I'm going into the office early every day and not finishing until quite late. By the time the weekend comes, I'm exhausted!

I shouldn't complain, though, because I'm actually really enjoying the work. It's challenging but interesting, and the pay rise means that Ania and I can actually afford to buy a house now.

We found one we really liked and put in an offer. Unfortunately, the seller received a higher offer and so accepted that. We were really disappointed but it was a bit further away than we had wanted so we're hoping to find something similar but a little closer.

³What have you been up to recently? Any interesting news?

All the best,

Danny

5 Read the Focus box and check your answers in Exercise 4.

6 Rewrite the sentences with phrases in the Focus box.

1 Tell me about your recent news.
  What _____

2 The news about your neighbour is very sad.
  I'm _____

3 William has some news.
  Have _____

4 The news about your engagement is good.
  I'm _____

5 How's life in the big city?
  How _____

6 I heard that you broke your leg.
  I'm _____

7 Football has made me busy.
  I've _____

8 It's good that you're enjoying yourself on holiday.
  Sounds _____

7 Which sentence or question is more informal, a or b?

1 a I am writing to inform you that I won a competition.
  b As for me, I've recently won a competition!

2 a Have you heard the news about the football team?
  b I would like to know if you've heard the news about the football team.

3 a It is with great sadness that we heard about your grandmother.
  b I'm so sorry to hear about your grandmother.

4 a We were delighted to hear the news about your promotion.
  b We're really pleased to hear about your promotion.

Prepare

8 You're going to write a reply to Danny and give him your news. Use the following structure to plan your email.

> Greeting _____
> React to Danny's good news _____
>
> React to Danny's bad news _____
>
> Answer Danny's question _____
>
> Give some news of your own – good, bad or both
> _____
>
> Sign off _____

Write

9 Write your email. Use your plan in Exercise 8 to help you. Remember to use an informal tone.

10 Use the following questions to help you edit your email.
- Have you reacted to Danny's news?
- Have you used a clear structure?
- Have you used an informal tone?

Grammar

Past perfect simple and continuous

1 **Choose the correct alternatives.**

1 By the time we got to the café, they *stopped*/*'d stopped* serving food.

2 I sat down and started reading the book that I'd just *bought*/*been buying*.

3 The TV series that we'd *watched*/*been watching* for weeks had a disappointing ending.

4 The sun *had been shining*/*shone* all day, so we were disappointed when it went in.

5 I *never*/*'d never* heard of the band that were playing on the radio before.

6 We didn't get into the match even though we *were*/*'d been* queueing for hours.

7 Tom had already *ordered*/*been ordering* some food by the time I arrived.

8 Paula went to bed early because she *worked*/*had been working* for over 12 hours.

2 **Complete the text with the correct form of the verbs in brackets.**

A vivid memory. But whose?

Memories are strange. I have one memory that I can recall really clearly from when I was six. I lived with my parents in the small, terraced house that they ¹_____ (buy) just after I was born. I went outside to play on my scooter. I remember that it ²_____ (rain) for hours so I soon got wet but I didn't mind. After I ³_____ (ride) around for a little while, the woman next door invited me in. She wanted me to try some of the cake she ⁴_____ (just/make). In fact, she ⁵_____ (bake) all day and ⁶_____ (make) several different types of cake. I picked the chocolate one and she cut me a slice.

While I ate, the woman showed me photos that her son ⁷_____ (sent) of her grandchildren. Her son ⁸_____ (already/move) to Australia by the time his children were born so she ⁹_____ (never/meet) them. I think she was sad about that.

Anyway, I put the last bite of cake in my mouth and started choking. I couldn't breathe and started to panic. Fortunately, the woman ¹⁰_____ (be) a nurse so knew exactly what to do. She turned me upside down and hit me on my back. The cake fell out and I could breathe again.

So, why is this memory strange? Well, it's really clear in my mind, so much so that it feels like it happened yesterday. And yet, the funny thing is, I don't actually remember it, but I've been told the story so many times by my mum, that I feel I like do.

Vocabulary

Memory

3 **Complete the sentences with the correct form of the words in the box.**

forget	memorable	memorise
memory (x2)	mind	recall	remind

1 I have a good _____ for faces but I never remember people's names.

2 Your perfume _____ me of those pink flowers in our garden.

3 I have to _____ all of these words before my English test next week.

4 I can still _____ the first day I met you.

5 What did we have for lunch? I've got no _____ of it at all!

6 I loved our wedding. It was such a _____ day.

7 When you visit Grandad, bear in _____ that he's not very well.

8 Don't _____ to buy Mum a birthday present.

4 **Complete the conversations using the prompts in brackets and other words you need.**

1 A: _____ (you / recall / name) of that hotel we stayed in last week?
   B: The King's Hotel, I think.

2 A: _____ (this music / remind you / anything)?
   B: No, why? Should it?

3 A: Well, _____ (that meeting / memorable).
   B: Yes, it was but for all the wrong reasons!

4 A: How come you can remember my mobile number but I can't?
   B: _____ (I / always / good / memory / numbers).

5 A: _____ (I / will / never / forget / time) that you called the teacher 'Dad'.
   B: Oh yes – that was so embarrassing!

6 A: We had this same conversation last week.
   B: Did we? _____ (I / no memory / it at all). Sorry!

7 A: _____ (None of us / need / memorise / history dates) any more.
   B: You're right. We can just look them up online!

Vocabulary
Character adjectives

1 Read the descriptions. What adjective describes each person? The first letter is given to help you.

1 Steve thinks he's better than everyone and can be quite unpleasant.
   a_____

2 The new receptionist is really sweet but she clearly lacks knowledge and skills.
   i_____

3 Alan always thinks about how he can make people happy. **t**_____

4 My nephew's achieved so much in his life. He's a really surprising guy. **r**_____

5 The boss can be very strong.
   t_____

6 You never know what my friend Matt will do next. **u**_____

7 Rachel feels sure that her job interview will go well. **c**_____

8 I want to go to New Zealand and I won't let anything stop me! **d**_____

2 Complete the conversations with the adjectives in the box.

> arrogant   bold   competitive
> determined   reasonable   remarkable
> stubborn   thoughtful

1 **A:** I hear what you're saying but I won't change my mind.
   B: Oh, don't be so _____!

2 **A:** I just walked straight into my boss's office and asked for more money.
   B: Wow, that was _____ of you.

3 **A:** You don't need to be so _____ all the time.
   B: You know me. I hate to lose.

4 **A:** I got you a coffee from the shop. Milk and one sugar, right?
   B: Yes, that's really _____, thanks.

5 **A:** Jenny wants the report by midday.
   B: What? That's crazy – she's usually very _____.

6 **A:** I'm _____ to get fit this year.
   B: Well, if you put your mind to it, then you can do it.

7 **A:** Eva got an A in all her subjects this year.
   B: I'm not surprised. She's a _____ woman.

8 **A:** If anyone should get the job, it's me.
   B: Don't be so _____! The others are good workers, too.

Grammar
Comparatives and superlatives

3 Choose the correct alternatives.

1 Russia is *by far/a lot* bigger than China.
2 The longer we waited, the *more/much* impatient we became.
3 This film adaptation isn't as good *as/than* the original.
4 This is *by far/far more* the best steak I've ever eaten.
5 It's not *as warm/warmer* today as it was yesterday.
6 You're not *less/lesser* of a man if you cry at films!
7 This mobile phone is the *least/less* reliable one I've ever had.
8 We have to walk *much more/so much* quickly or we'll be late.

4 Complete the text with one word in each gap.

> **The cola wars**
> Coca Cola and Pepsi are by **1**_____ the most well-known business rivals when it comes to soft drinks. Coca Cola was invented in 1886, 12 years earlier **2**_____ Pepsi. It was already selling millions of litres a year when Pepsi appeared. Pepsi wanted a share of that market and the companies have been **3**_____ best of rivals ever since.
> Their rivalry became much **4**_____ famous in the 1970s when Pepsi introduced the Pepsi Challenge. They asked customers to blind taste Coke and Pepsi and say which they preferred. Pepsi say that over 50 percent of people chose their drink. Whether that was **5**_____ little over 50 percent or **6**_____ more than 50 percent, we can't be sure. However, this started an era of competition known as the *cola wars*. **7**_____ harder Coca Cola promoted their company, the greater the effort Pepsi made and vice versa. It's still clear today that they're as competitive **8**_____ each other when it comes to selling their products and this is unlikely to change any time soon.

5 Complete the second sentence so it means the same as the first.

1 You're better at languages than me.
   I'm not _____ at languages _____ you.

2 That exercise wasn't as easy as I'd expected.
   That exercise _____ difficult _____ I'd expected.

3 I've never had such a fast car.
   This is by _____ car I've ever had.

4 The blue shirt is nicer than the green one.
   The green shirt _____ the blue one.

5 I feel much more relaxed today.
   I feel a _____ stressed _____ yesterday.

6 When I feel more tired, I sleep less.
   _____ I feel, _____ I sleep.

7 You don't look awake enough to work today.
   You look far _____ to work today.

8 The Bears played much worse than The Tigers and still won!
   The Bears didn't _____ The Tigers and still won!

Vocabulary
Arguments

1 Match the sentence halves.

1 Neither of us agree so we have to find ......
2 I love your idea but I have ......
3 I know you're trying to pick ......
4 None of my family see eye ......
5 Eduardo will often back ......
6 There's clearly an underlying ......
7 My friend Anne and I clash ......
8 If I say *black*, my boyfriend will immediately ......

a a fight with me but I won't argue with you.
b an issue with some of the details.
c contradict me and say *white*. It's infuriating!
d down if you give him good reasons why you disagree with him.
e issue as to why the Brown brothers fight all the time.
f to eye on politics.
g with each other on parenting issues all the time.
h a compromise.

2 Complete the conversation with sentences a–g.

.ıll 16:24 50% 🔋

Emma
Are you coming out tonight?

Lucy
No sorry. Going to get an early night.

Emma
You had an early night last night!

Lucy
I know, but Ivan will be there. ¹ ......

Emma
He doesn't. He likes you.

Lucy
² ......

Emma
Because he likes talking to you!

Lucy
No, he doesn't! ³ ......

Emma
He enjoys a good argument. ⁴ ......

Lucy
Are you sure about that? He gets so annoyed with me and he's so stubborn. ⁵ ......

Emma
I honestly think he just likes a good argument. ⁶ ...... Besides, there'll be plenty of us there so you won't need to speak to him.

Lucy
Alright, I'll come. ⁷ ......

a That's why he contradicts you.
b He seems to have an issue with me.
c We clash on almost every subject.
d He never backs down.
e But he picks a fight with me every time I see him.
f But promise me you'll intervene if he starts a fight!
g There's no underlying issue there.

Language focus
Forming adjectives

3 Complete the table with the correct form of the words in the box. Some words go in more than one section.

accept	adapt	allergy	colour	ethics	fool
history	logic	meat	nightmare	outrage	point
ridicule	scare	use			

-al	-ful	-ic	-ish

-less	-ous	-able/-ible	-y

4 Complete the adjectives in the sentences.

1 Fixing this won't be easy but it's do...... .
2 Today's crossword is really trick...... .
3 So, what's a tradition...... meal in your country?
4 I love this film. It's a class...... .
5 Everyone loves Vera. She's just so like...... .
6 You don't think that snake's poison...... , do you?
7 The way Tom calls his dad 'Sir' is so respect...... .
8 Please remember that this information is confident...... .

5 Complete the text with the correct form of the words in the box.

accident	apology	delight	disrespect	night
point	reason	sense		

We had an issue with one of our neighbours. It was our fault at first. We put some weedkiller on our drive and unfortunately her cat ate some and got sick. Luckily, the cat got better. We were really ¹ ...... and, after paying for the vet's bills, we thought that would be the end of it. After all, our neighbour had always seemed entirely ² .... We were wrong.

The next month, we came home to find that someone had driven across our front garden and over our ³ ...... rose bushes. We thought it was ⁴ ...... at first, but when it happened again and again, we knew someone was doing it on purpose. Eventually, someone saw our neighbour doing it. We tried to have a ⁵ ...... conversation with her about it several times but she was just completely ⁶ ...... to us. In the end, it was ⁷ ....

We lived with this for over a year before we moved away because of work. We weren't sorry to say goodbye. The whole situation had been ⁸ ....

Vocabulary

Adjectives to describe food

1 **Which food is the odd one out in each group?**

1 spicy:
curry, bread, salsa, chilli pepper
....

2 creamy:
yoghurt, ice cream, full fat milk, fruit juice
....

3 crunchy:
cheese, pepper, carrot, nuts
....

4 greasy:
chips, cauliflower, fried chicken, crisps
....

5 salty:
crisps, instant noodles, cheese, tomatoes
....

2 **Complete the sentences with the adjectives in the box.**

bland   creamy   crunchy   filling
greasy   raw   salty   tough

1 I don't like .... fish. I prefer
it cooked.

2 That soup was really ....
I'm so full!

3 This beef is very .... I can hardly
get my knife through it.

4 This dessert is so .... that it's
making me feel a bit sick.

5 Your burger looks really ....
It's swimming in fat!

6 I put hot sauce on everything. I hate
.... food.

7 Processed food is often really
.... It's not good for you.

8 Lettuce should be .... , not soft
like this stuff.

English in action

Complain and give and respond to feedback

3 **Complete the conversations using the prompts in brackets.**

1 **Customer:** Sorry, could we cancel our desserts? ....
.... (We / be / somewhere / 15 minutes).
Waiter: Sure, no problem.

2 **Customer:** ....
(this soup / supposed / cold)?
Waiter: Yes, it is. It's gazpacho, a cold soup.

3 **Customer:** Excuse me, ...
.... (I / ask / chips / but / got mashed potato).
Waiter: I'm sorry about that, madam. I'll bring you some chips.

4 **Customer:** Our food's taking some time. ....
.... (you / check / order / me)?
Waiter: Of course, sir. I'll do it now.

5 **Customer:** ....
(this steak / tough). I'm afraid I can't eat it.
Waiter: I'm sorry about that, sir, but our other customers like it.
Customer: Well, that's not good enough. ....
.... (I / speak to / manager)?

4 **Put the words in the correct order to make sentences.**

1 a big / service / gets / thumbs up / The
....

2 strong / one of / Your cakes / your / are / points
....

3 bear / you / in mind / Perhaps / the feedback / could
....

4 might / Your staff / a bit more / to try / polite / want / being
....

5 the food / Overall, / felt that / people / good / was
....

6 on board / that / take / I'll
....

5 **Complete the conversation with phrases a–h.**

Researcher: So, here are the results of the survey we carried out with
your customers. OK. **1**...... the feedback was positive.
Manager: Oh, good. That's a relief!
Researcher: **2**...... your quick service and friendly customer service team.
Manager: Great! We work hard to offer a good service.
Researcher: And that's clear to customers. However, **3**...... the quality of
your bedroom furniture isn't as good as it should be.
Manager: Oh, right. Well, **4**......, it's the cheapest furniture we offer so
the quality is going to be lower.
Researcher: **5**...... offering higher quality bedroom furniture, too?
Manager: OK, **6**...... .
Researcher: That was **7**...... . Actually, it was the only complaint.
Everything else **8**...... .
Manager: Great!

a from my point of view
b Customers appreciate
c I'll take that on board
d The first thing to say is that

e got a big thumbs up
f the biggest complaint
g Perhaps you could look at
h some people felt that

Reading

1 Read the article. What's the writer's overall opinion?

  a Rivalry produces only positive effects.

  b Rivalry can be beneficial if you watch out for the negative effects.

  c Rivalry has a much more negative impact than positive.

2 Read the article again. Are the sentences true (T) or false (F)?

  1 Rivalry makes you put in more effort.

  2 Rivalry shows you what you can and can't do.

  3 A rival is usually someone we can't stand.

  4 Rivalry reduces levels of motivation.

  5 Rivalry causes people to be dishonest.

  6 Rivalry pushes us to notice every competitor.

3 In which paragraphs can you find this information?

  1 We make decisions about a rival based on emotions, not facts.

  2 A rival can help you recognise what you are best at.

  3 A lack of sports rivalry might reduce the amount of preparation players do.

  4 Rivalry forces you to reach goals that you did not think possible.

  5 An unknown company beat two existing companies to a new product.

  6 A rival is someone in a similar position or situation to us.

  7 Businesses can't succeed long-term without thinking of new ideas.

  8 Rivalry causes athletes to increase their speed.

  9 Understanding what skills you lack is essential to personal development.

  10 It is important not to let your desire to succeed have a negative impact on your behaviour.

  11 Current rivals are not the only people we are competing against.

  12 Some companies have lied about competitors in order to get ahead.

4 Choose the correct alternatives.

  1 In paragraph 1, the writer creates a picture of enemies in the reader's mind to *present / reject* this idea of rivalry.

  2 The writer uses a mirror in paragraph 2 to describe *hiding / revealing* something about a person.

  3 When the writer says 'don't go down the route of' in paragraph 5, he means *decide to act in a particular way / go to a particular place*.

5 Find the words and phrases in the box in the article. Then, match them with definitions 1–8.

> challenge (v) cheat dominate drive someone to do something
> innovative motivated strengths weaknesses

  1 strongly influence someone to do something

  2 test your skills and abilities

  3 abilities that gives you an advantage

  4 lack of strengths, power or skills

  5 new, different and better than existed before

  6 behave dishonestly to win or get an advantage

  7 keen to do something

  8 control

6 Complete the sentences with the correct form of the words and phrases in Exercise 5. There is one word or phrase that you do not need.

  1 Don't just focus on what you're good at, consider your _____, too.

  2 His rival has accused him of _____ his way to the top.

  3 It's important _____ yourself and try new ways of working.

  4 The company _____ the industry for the last ten years.

  5 Your honesty is one of your greatest _____ .

  6 The _____ design set them apart from their rivals.

  7 In order to succeed, you must be highly _____ .

7 Complete the sentences with words in the article. Find collocations in the article to help you.

  1 A rival can push you to achieve _____ grades.

  2 A company can only achieve _____ success if it creates new products or services.

  3 If we want to win, we have to make _____ improvements.

  4 Rivalry can _____ affect motivation.

  5 Rivalry in sport results in _____ levels of play.

  6 If you want to win in sport, you have to train _____ .

Rivalry: friend or foe?

[1]The word rivalry brings to mind images of enemies fighting it out to the death but it doesn't need to be that way. Rivalry can be really beneficial. It can push you to work harder and drive you to achieve things you couldn't imagine that you could achieve. In the workplace, a rival might encourage you to get a promotion you didn't think possible. At school, it might challenge you to achieve higher grades. On the playing field, it might push you to run faster or tackle harder. In business, it certainly pushes companies to be more creative and more innovative, both vital for continued success.

[2]A rival can also hold a mirror up to you and show you both your strengths and your weaknesses. The rival makes you think about what you do well and therefore what you need to continue doing. They also show you what you do less well and what you need to work on. None of us like to know about the things we're not good at, but we do need to understand our weaknesses to be able to make the necessary improvements to become even stronger and more successful.

[3]Of course, a rival is not just someone we work with, study with or compete against on the sports field. It's not even someone we dislike. A rival is someone we may respect very much, but about whom we're unable to be objective. Our rivalry becomes personal because we want to win so much. It could be another student whose grades are as good as ours. It might be a colleague who wants the same promotion as us or a sports team who we need to beat to win the cup. Rivalry expert Dr Gavin Kilduff defines a rival as someone with whom we have a lot in common. It's also someone that we compete against regularly and feel competitive towards.

[4]In his research, Dr Kilduff found that runners were motivated to run as much as 25 seconds faster in a 5K race where a rival was competing. It's clear that rivalry can significantly affect motivation. We can see this happen in professional sports. Rivalries such as that between tennis players Roger Federer and Rafael Nadal, and more recently Novak Djokovic, have resulted in incredibly high levels of tennis. Without that rivalry, those players may not train so hard or compete so determinedly.

[5]Of course, rivalry has its downsides, too. Our desperation to beat our rival can cause us to lie or cheat to get what we want. There are cases of businesses who try to sabotage the success of a competitor by spreading false information, for example. While their actions may not exactly be illegal, they're certainly immoral. We need to be sure that we don't go down the route of negative actions.

[6]Another possible side effect of rivalry is the fact that we can be so focused on our rival that we don't see other competitors close behind us. An example of this is two long-standing soft drinks companies who were so focused on each other that a new company came out of nowhere with a completely new drink that is now world-leading. So, we should always pay attention to that new runner in the race, employee at work or student in the class because we never know when they might step up and beat us.

Listening

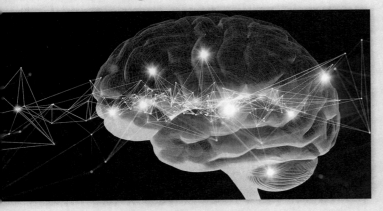

1 🔊 **3.01 Listen to a talk about memories. What's the main point the speaker is making?**
  a Scientists now believe that our memories change over time.
  b Scientists are doing studies to find out how memories are stored.
  c Scientists have discovered where our brain creates memories.

2 Listen again. Choose the correct option a, b or c.
  1 Paul says that memories ....
    a are fixed in the past.
    b are easy to understand.
    c define who we are.
  2 Memories are activated ....
    a in one special area of our minds.
    b across multiple parts of the brain.
    c using all of our senses.
  3 Studies have shown that our memories are affected by ....
    a our emotions.
    b incorrect facts.
    c other people's memories.
  4 What does Paul say about our knowledge of memory? ....
    a We know a lot about how it works.
    b We're slowly learning more about it.
    c We will never completely understand it.
  5 Scientists now think that a memory changes ....
    a each time we remember it.
    b when we actively lie about it.
    c depending on our feeling when it was created.
  6 Scientists previously thought that memories ....
    a were permanently fixed once created.
    b continued to change as we got older.
    c changed for only for a brief time.

3 Which statement about memories might the speaker agree with?
  1 They provide us with facts about the past.
  2 Scientists are now sure about how they work.
  3 We shouldn't rely on them for factual information.

Writing

1 Read the anecdote and choose the best title for it.
  a A waste of courage
  b A tragic mistake
  c A disappointing meeting

2 Read the anecdote again and choose the correct alternatives.

I was travelling on the New York subway **1**_not so long ago/ nowadays_ when I noticed this man standing near me. I knew he was someone famous but I couldn't remember who he was. I thought hard **2**_for about two stops/over time_. Then, **3**_all of a sudden/eventually_ it came to me. It was Matt Damon! I couldn't believe it! I mean, it's not every day you get so close to a real-life Hollywood actor; a superstar even. I looked around but no one else seemed to have noticed. I tried to catch another passenger's eye but everyone was either looking elsewhere or reading a book.

I didn't know what to do. I'm not a very bold person and I didn't want to disturb him, but this was a once in a lifetime opportunity. So **4**_in the end/the following day_, I stood up, walked over to Mr Damon and said 'I really enjoy your films, it's great to meet you.' He looked quite surprised but smiled all the same and agreed to take a selfie with me. By now everyone was looking at us and I felt quite brave. **5**_After a few minutes/As soon as_ of polite chat, I thanked Mr Damon, got off at the next stop and went back to my friend's place. I couldn't wait until she got home from work so I could show off the photo of my new-found friend. **6**_In the meantime/After hours_, I posted it online for my friends back home to see with the caption 'Look at me being brave!' Imagine my embarrassment when they all pointed out it wasn't Matt Damon at all, just someone who looked a bit similar.

3 Match the phrases in the box with uses 1–4. Read the Focus box to check your answers.

> after a few hours all of a sudden as soon as
> eventually in 2019 in the meantime meanwhile
> nowadays over time the following day

1 Show when something happened

_____

2 Show how much time passed

_____

3 Show that two events happened at the same time

_____

4 Show how quickly the event happened

_____

Timing and sequencing past events

Certain words and phrases tell us about the timing and sequence of events in the past.

Showing when something happened
This was **in early 2018** and I was visiting a friend.
I was travelling on the New York subway **not so long ago** when …
**Nowadays** I never approach strangers, famous or otherwise!

Showing how much time passed
**Over time** I'd become bolder.
**The following day** I admitted that I'd made a mistake.
**After a few minutes of** chatting …

Showing that two events happened at the same time
**In the meantime**, I posted it online.

Showing how quickly the event happened
**All of a sudden**, it came to me.
**Eventually**, I got back to my friend's place.
**As soon as** I introduced myself, he smiled.
**In the end**, I stood up.

4 Choose the correct alternatives.

1 I wasn't confident in my job at first but _after days/ over time_ I became bolder.

2 It took a long time to get home but _meanwhile/ eventually_, I got there.

3 I went travelling across Asia _in early 2016/nowadays_.

4 We ordered food _as soon as/in the end_ we arrived.

5 Our plane wasn't due to leave until 9 p.m. so _in the meantime/not so long ago_, we had a drink.

6 _Nowadays/All of a sudden_ I don't go out much but things were different in my 20s.

7 _Over time/After hours_ of waiting for the bus, we gave up and walked home.

8 She gave me the worst haircut of my life. _The following day/As soon as_, I went back and complained.

5 Complete the text with the phrases in the box.

> all of a sudden as soon as eventually in late 2014
> in the meantime nowadays

This happened **1** _____ . I'd just got off a train and was walking towards the exit of the station. **2** _____ , I heard a woman scream with frustration so I turned round to see what was happening. To the side of me was a woman fighting over a laptop bag with a large man. Clearly, he was trying to steal her bag. A couple of people ran to get help. **3** _____ , I ran over and grabbed the bag myself. I pulled in the same direction as the woman and **4** _____ the man let go and fell backwards onto the ground. The woman smiled at me, took the bag and, rather strangely, ran off. I expected the man to run away himself but he didn't. In fact, **5** _____ the police arrived, he walked over to them and calmly explained that a woman had just stolen his laptop. I felt awful and was very glad when the police realised it was just a misunderstanding on my part. Needless to say, I don't help out strangers in need **6** _____ without fully understanding the situation first!

Prepare

6 You're going to write an anecdote for a blog post. Think about a time that you were bold or made a mistake. Make notes about:
- when it was
- where it was
- who was involved
- what happened
- how you and other people reacted
- how you felt
- what happened in the end

7 Use your ideas in Exercise 6 to plan your anecdote. What phrases in the Focus box can you use?

Write

8 Write your anecdote. Use timing and sequencing phrases to help the reader understand when things happened.

Vocabulary
Adjectives to describe things

1 Reorder the letters to make words that match the definitions.

  1 light and thin, or not strong or well-made
    myslfi

  2 thick, solid and heavy   *khuycn*

  3 shaped like an egg   *alvo*

  4 shining in small, bright flashes   *ksrapyl*

  5 shaped with four sides, two of which are longer   *lcratenagur*

  6 fashionable, expensive and made by a well-known creator   *gndersie*

  7 extremely valuable   *celspirse*

  8 exactly the same   *cldinteia*

2 Put the adjectives in brackets in the correct place in the texts.

'I inherited this fruit bowl from my grandma when she died. It's not worth any money, but it's **1**_____ to me because it reminds me of my grandparents. I don't use it for fruit. It's just **2**_____ but I think it looks really **3**_____ in my living room.'
(decorative, elegant, priceless)

'I've got a pair of **4**_____ boots that I absolutely love. They're not just bright, though. They're also **5**_____! They're **6**_____ so they cost me a lot of money but I just had to have them.'
(designer, sparkly, vivid-pink)

'I saw these paintings in a second-hand shop and knew I had to get them. They're **7**_____, which is unusual for landscape paintings, and the frames are really **8**_____. People think the paintings are **9**_____ but there are some differences between them if you look carefully. That's why I like them. You can play 'spot the difference' with them!'
(chunky, identical, oval)

3 Put the words in order to make sentences and questions. Add a comma if necessary.

  1 big / need a / with that dress / you / necklace / chunky

  2 bedsheets / these / flimsy / hate / cheap / I

  3 plastic / you got / small / any of those / have / plates ?

  4 round / never seen / face / huge / a watch / I've / with such a

  5 wears / cotton / designer / only ever / Manu / shirts

  6 very / are / gold / those / earrings / elegant

Grammar
Relative clauses

4 Put the words in brackets in the correct place in the sentences. Add a relative pronoun and commas if necessary.

  1 I really enjoyed that book on psychology.   (you lent me)

  2 My parents are both retired.   (now live in Spain)

  3 I met a woman today.   (works with you)

  4 The museum is called The Williamson.   (you're talking about)

  5 My phone isn't working.   (I only got last year)

  6 I helped a man last night.   (car had broken down)

5 Join the two sentences. Add a relative pronoun if necessary.

  1 That's the bus driver. I had an argument with him this morning.

  2 Susanne is a doctor. Her children go to school with mine.

  3 The restaurant's in Gold Street. It's in the east of the city.

  4 William's sister Jenny has just got a big promotion. She works in marketing.

  5 I'm so sorry but I left the umbrella on the metro. You lent it to me.

  6 My flat is in a pretty nice area of the town. It overlooks the park.

6 Complete the article with clauses a–g. Add a relative pronoun before each clause.

Art or not?

The band KLF was one of the biggest selling bands in the UK in the early 1990s. The two band members, **1**_____, were well-known for their stage performances. However, it was a performance of a different kind that got people talking.

On 23 August, 1991, the band took a boat out to Jura, **2**_____. With them, they took £1 million in cash, **3**_____. They then built a fire and burnt the money. The film **4**_____ has caused a lot of discussion over the years. For some people, it was art. For many others, it was money **5**_____ and that other people deserved more.

Neither of the band members have explained exactly why they did it. They believe it's an act **6**_____. However, one of the pair, **7**_____, has since said that he has some regrets about it.

  a is an island off the coast of Scotland

  b people should be allowed to interpret differently

  c were very creative

  d they took while doing this

  e was most of their earnings

  f children were very shocked when they heard the story

  g was completely wasted

Vocabulary

Job requirements

1 Match the sentence halves.

1 Ana has a background ....
2 You need at least two years' ....
3 Francesco has strong communication ....
4 My brother has a flair ....
5 Actors have to be able to cope ....
6 Everyone in my family is fluent ....

a skills as a manager.
b with criticism.
c in physics.
d for languages so picks them up really fast.
e in two languages.
f experience for this job.

2 Complete the conversation with phrases using the words in brackets.

A: I hear you're interested in becoming a food scientist.

B: Yes. I ¹ .... (flair) cooking and I ² .... (passion) science so they seem to go well together.

A: Well, you'll need to
³ .... (degree) food science.

B: I know. I've already started looking at degree courses. I'm studying sciences and I've got two years'
⁴ .... (experience) working in restaurants which should help.

A: Good. Food scientists need to
⁵ .... (critical thinking skills) and a knowledge of food manufacturing. You could try to get some work experience.

B: That's a good idea. That way, I could find out if I like it and if I would be able to
⁶ .... (cope) it.

A: ⁷ .... (willing) give up some of your summer holidays for that?

B: Sure. I ⁸ .... (bothered) losing a couple of weeks.

Grammar

Obligation and prohibition

3 Complete the text with one word in each gap.

> ### Job search: how times have changed
> Getting a job has changed considerably over the last two decades. If you wanted to find a job previously, you had ¹ .... look for ads in a newspaper. You ² .... required to print out your CV and then you ³ .... to post it. These days, you can just look for ads online and then email your CV. Easy! However, no employer ⁴ .... to read through hundreds or thousands of applications. Apparently, a computer does it for them. Another difference is that you ⁵ .... have to have quite so many skills in the past. Technology skills, for example, ⁶ .... required for most jobs but today they're essential. You've also ⁷ .... to know how to use social media in order to network, but of course you ⁸ .... be careful about what you post online. In the past, you didn't ⁹ .... to worry about your employer seeing photos of your last birthday party online, but that's not true anymore!

4 Correct the mistakes in five of the sentences.

1 I have to leave in five minutes for my dentist's appointment.

2 You don't have to eat in here. It's forbidden.

3 Jamie's got to go to the next meeting but I didn't have to.

4 All guests are required to wear formal dress at the event.

5 We weren't needed to stay up late when we were kids.

6 I've got to go out and buy some milk for breakfast.

7 You mustn't call me tomorrow but you can if you want.

8 Alison doesn't have to go to work yesterday.

5 Rewrite the sentences using the words in capital letters so they mean the same.

1 It's necessary for us to get up early tomorrow. **HAVE**
....

2 I was prohibited from going out alone at night when I was a child. **ALLOWED**
....

3 It wasn't necessary for Sara to go into work early, but she did anyway. **REQUIRED**
....

4 It's really necessary for you to see a dentist about your tooth. **MUST**
....

5 You're prohibited from bringing your own food into the cinema. **CAN'T**
....

6 It's not necessary for David to come to the meeting. **NEED**
....

7 It's necessary to pay more attention to me when I'm speaking! **GOT**
....

8 It really wasn't necessary for you to bring me a present. **HAVE**
....

Vocabulary
21st-century words

1 **What is each person describing? The first letter is given to help you.**

1 You take it yourself and then put it online for everyone to see.
   s_____

2 It's when you put a word into a search engine to look for information online. **g**_____

3 I don't understand the meaning of all these little yellow faces you send me. **e**_____

4 It's a joke that spreads online, usually a photo with some text on it or a video. **m**_____

5 You don't need to enter your PIN number. You just pay by waving your card over the machine. **c**_____

6 Stop sending me silly messages or I'll take you off my list of contacts.
   u_____

2 **Complete the sentences by joining words in box A with words in box B. Make sure the new wordor phrase is in the correct form.**

A	binge- crowd hash pay time- virtual

B	assistant poor source tag wall watch

1 I'm sure my _____ listens to my conversations. Ads pop up on my phone for things I've mentioned to my friends.

2 My roommate and I spent all weekend _____ a really terrible reality TV show. We couldn't stop!

3 If you need money for your business idea, you could _____ it online.

4 I'm really _____ at the moment. There just aren't enough hours in the day.

5 Just go on Twitter and search for _____ ManUtd if you want to know the latest score.

6 The article you sent me is behind a _____ , but I don't want to take out a subscription.

3 **Choose the correct option a, b or c.**

A: Have you seen this **¹**____? It's the photo of the cat and the cucumber.

B: Oh, that's really old. I used to send that same image as an **²**____. It's a lot funnier when the cat moves.

A: I haven't got round to sending animations yet. I'm still trying to work out what all the **³**____ on my keyboard mean. So many different smiley faces!

B: You'll get used to them. Oh, can you believe how many **⁴**____ Maxine has posted today? Almost the same picture of her face each time.

A: I know what you mean. I've actually **⁵**____ her so I don't see them anymore.

B: I might have to do the same. I'm **⁶**____ – I can't afford to waste hours looking at her different hairstyles all day.

1	a	selfie	b	emoji	c	meme
2	a	animated gif	b	virtual tour	c	hashtag
3	a	paywalls	b	hashtags	c	emojis
4	a	emojis	b	selfies	c	virtual assistants
5	a	googled	b	unfriended	c	crowdsourced
6	a	time-poor	b	tech-savvy	c	contactless

Language focus
Forming verbs with *en*

4 **Choose the correct alternatives.**

1 I love your smile. It *brightens/ softens* my day.

2 These trousers are too long. Could you *lengthen/ shorten* them for me?

3 It *saddens/ worsens* me to know there are poor children in the world.

4 Cook the onions before adding the other vegetables so they *soften/ weaken*.

5 Can you *broaden/ enlarge* the photo on your screen? It's too small.

6 Who's going to *enforce/ enrage* the new copyright laws?

5 **Complete the text with the correct form of the words in capital letters.**

Is a cashless society desirable?

The need for cash is **¹**_____ each year as more and more of us use technology to pay our way. Methods of payment seem to **²**_____ regularly – contactless, mobile technology and online. Many predict that we'll have a cashless society before long, but will this **³**_____ our lives or make it more difficult?

For many of us, it'll improve our lives. No one will need to carry cash around and the time we take to pay for things will **⁴**_____ . On the other hand, a cashless society will **⁵**_____ the day-to-day routine for those of us without bank accounts or phones. Cash enables these people to function. We need to **⁶**_____ that they can continue to do that in a cashless society.

LESS

BROAD

RICH

SHORT

DANGER

SURE

Listening

1 🔊 **4.01 Listen to a conversation between three friends about mobile phones. Which of these things do they discuss?**

- Being without your phone
- Design features of mobile phones
- Losing contact with people online
- Taking a break from social media
- Trying a new app
- Ways of using social media

2 Listen again. Are the sentences true (T) or false (F)?

1 A digital detox means being offline for a period of time. _____
2 Mara is offline all the time outside of work. _____
3 James is able to stop himself from looking at messages that arrive. _____
4 Dopamine is released in our brains when we send a message. _____
5 Designers create phone software that encourages constant use. _____
6 James never watches the three dots when on social media. _____
7 A research project was stopped to protect the participants. _____
8 Nomophobia describes being afraid of mobile phones. _____

3 Listen again and answer the questions with between one and three words.

1 Mara is fed up of looking at photos of babies and what else? _____
2 What kind of programme did Mara binge-watch last weekend? _____
3 What does James say he wouldn't be able to cope without? _____
4 What has Mara started doing since she gave up social media? _____
5 What does James say is hard to do when your phone makes a noise? _____
6 James compares feeling good when a message arrives to what? _____
7 How does Mara say we feel when we wait for three dots to turn into a message _____
8 According to scientists, what is losing your phone similar to losing? _____

4 Match the words in bold with meanings a–f.

1 When we get a message, our body **releases** a chemical into our brains. _____
2 Designers encourage us to use their apps by including **features** like those three little dots. _____
3 The three dots promise a reward which **causes** our brains to produce dopamine. _____
4 I love my social media but that's a bit **extreme**! _____
5 Separation anxiety is something more and more of us are **suffering from**. _____
6 Are we really so **desperate** to keep in touch with people? _____

a unreasonable
b makes something happen
c needing or wanting something very much
d lets a substance flow out
e experience an unpleasant or difficult experience
f something you notice because it's important or attractive

5 Which person do you think says each thing? Choose the correct alternatives.

1 I tried a digital detox. I was wrong. I do suffer from nomophobia! *Sophie/James*
2 I've started noticing the design features we talked about and how they persuade me to stay on my phone. *James/Mara*
3 I've done a lot of reading on this topic which is why I know quite a lot about it. *Mara/Sophie*
4 My two-week digital detox has been a success so I'm going to extend it. *James/Mara*
5 I need to stop taking my phone everywhere with me. It stops me sleeping at night, especially. *Mara/James*

Reading

1 **Read the article. Match the questions with the answers.**

a Who might find it hard to declutter?

b Why has decluttering become so popular lately?

c Does decluttering help to protect the environment?

d Does it appeal to a particular age group?

e Does recycling what we own impact us in a good way?

f How much of an effect can decluttering have on us?

DECLUTTERING: THE NEW HOME TREND

The decluttering trend – removing unnecessary items from your home – has grown dramatically over the last few years. Here, we ask home expert Mariana Field to explain the reasons behind the trend and how decluttering can benefit us all.

Q: **1** ....

A: We're a materialistic society, constantly buying things to try to enrich our lives. However, we've begun to realise that we don't really need all those objects, especially as we end up throwing them into the back of a cupboard after a few months. Our days are busy and our homes are full. We're all looking to simplify our lives and that includes our homes. Current reality TV shows on the topic of decluttering both reflect the trend and contribute to bringing it to the average viewer's attention.

Q: **2** ....

A: Not especially, but different generations might have different reasons for doing it. For younger people, it tends to be about sustainability and an awareness of the impact material goods have on the environment. For those who are increasing in years, it's about downsizing. They want to move from their family home to a smaller one now their children have moved out.

Q: **3** ....

A: Well, I don't want to generalise, but people who remember a time when owning something was special. They can struggle to give things away because they worry that they might need it again in the future. Interestingly, in Sweden there's a trend towards decluttering as you get older so that you don't leave a house full of objects when you're gone which your children then have to sort out.

Q: **4** ....

A: It can be very good for our mental well-being. A clutter-free home can help us to relax and improve our relationships. We no longer fight because the remote control is lost under a sea of stuff! It can also improve our confidence. That might sound a little odd but we feel good when we set ourselves a goal and reach it. Decluttering is such a goal.

Q: **5** ....

A: It makes people aware of how much stuff they have. This can stop them from purchasing things they don't really need in the future which, of course, lessens the natural resources we use. Of course, some people simply spend money on new stuff to replace their old stuff but for others, they are able to keep their clutter down.

Q: **6** ....

A: It's making the best of a bad situation. It's great if someone else can enjoy something we no longer need because it lengthens its lifespan and stops them buying something new. But what if no one wants our old things? They go into landfill and sit in the ground for years, maybe decades, before they finally break down. And of course, transporting all our recycling from one place to another results in an increase of carbon emissions. So, it's better than nothing but it's not a long-term solution to the problem of sustainability.

2 Choose the correct option a, b or c.

1 According to Mariana Field, people declutter because they _____
  a are unable to find what they're looking for in their wardrobe.
  b want to encourage a less complicated way of life.
  c feel the need to copy what people do on television.

2 Mariana says that older people declutter in order to _____
  a reduce the size of their living space.
  b get rid of their children's old belongings.
  c reduce their impact on the environment.

3 Mariana believes that we feel good about ourselves when we _____
  a rest after spending time decluttering.
  b find unexpected items.
  c achieve a target.

4 Mariana says that decluttering helps the environment when people _____
  a change their buying habits.
  b replace old products with new products.
  c choose products that use fewer resources.

5 Mariana suggests that recycling _____
  a is the best way to deal with our materialistic ways.
  b addresses the issue of materialism to some degree.
  c prevents our material belongings from going to waste.

3 Find words in the article to match the definitions.

1 in a great and sudden way (introduction)
_____

2 all the time, or very often (paragraph 1)
_____

3 the effect or influence that something has on something else (paragraph 2)
_____

4 have to try hard to achieve something because something is difficult (paragraph 3)
_____

5 a feeling of having a happy and healthy mind (paragraph 4)
_____

6 the belief that you have the ability to do things well (paragraph 4)
_____

7 things in nature that we can use, e.g. trees, oil, etc. (paragraph 5)
_____

8 taking goods from one place to another using a vehicle (paragraph 6)
_____

4 What is the purpose of the article?

1 To persuade people to declutter their homes.
2 To inform the reader about different issues related to decluttering.
3 To criticise the impact that decluttering has on our lives.

5 Read people's tips on a forum about decluttering. Whose tip(s) refer(s) to ...

1 things you wear? _____ _____
2 keeping the number of items in your home the same? _____ _____
3 setting a target? _____ _____
4 something they saw on TV? _____
5 giving things to a second-hand shop? _____
6 physically marking when something has been achieved? _____
7 an activity that is designed to change your buying habits? _____
8 activities that the writer hasn't tried themselves? _____

Author	Comment
AdLib3	Start with a small goal and set a deadline, e.g. 'I'll clear out the hall cupboard by the end of next week.' When you do it, the sense of achievement motivates you to clear something else out. I can say this with experience!
Vichan	We have a 'one in one out' policy in our house. No one is allowed to bring anything new into the house before they donate something old to a charity shop. I'm talking about a toy, for example, not consumable goods like food!
Catty86	I saw something on a programme that I think could work. Turn all your coat hangers a particular way in your wardrobe. Every time you wear something, return it but put the coat hanger the opposite way. After six months, you can tell which clothes you haven't worn and get rid of them.
Hannah	I can't do anything without writing a list so that's where I start. I write down everything I want to sort out and tick each item off when it's done.
Linz99	Try living your life wearing only 30 items of clothing and 4 pairs of shoes over a month. You might need to increase the numbers a bit but it's mostly possible. It's a good reminder that we don't need to buy so many clothes which we stop wearing after just a few months.

6 Complete the sentences with words in the forum comments.

1 AdLib3 says that the satisfaction you feel when achieving a goal _____ you to do it again.
2 Vichan's family _____ an item to a charity every time they want to buy something new.
3 According to Catty86, a good way to _____ which clothes you wear is to hang them a certain way in the wardrobe after you wear them.
4 Hannah makes a list of things to do. Then, she can _____ each activity after she does it.
5 Linz99 suggests that wearing only 30 items of clothing and 4 pairs of shoes is a _____ that we don't need to own so many clothes.

Writing

1 Read the job advertisements and the email. Which job is the email writer applying for?

JOB OPENINGS

REPAIR TECHNICIANS

We're looking for a variety of repair technicians to mend broken furniture, electrical goods, watches and other possessions that customers bring to our *Bring things back to life* café. Our technicians must have:

- technical knowledge of their field, e.g. working with wood, electrics, ceramics, etc.
- a creative flair
- the ability to solve challenging problems
- attention to detail
- patience and determination
- an ability to show care and empathy for people's treasured possessions

Apply by emailing your CV to roberthall@bringthingsbacktolife.mail

CHIEF LISTENING OFFICER

We need a CLO to monitor discussions of our company on social media and to respond quickly to any form of criticism or misinformation. Our CLO will need to have a degree in business studies or marketing, have an excellent understanding of social media platforms, have excellent communication skills, good analytical skills and an ability to be persuasive.

Send your CV to Maddie Smith at HR@dentons.mail

To: roberthall@bringsthingsbacktolife.mail
Subject: Application for the position of Repair Technician

17th April

Dear Mr Hall,

I am writing to apply for the position of Repair Technician advertised on jobshare.com.

As you will see from my attached CV, I have ten years' experience in repairing furniture. **a** <u>I have a good eye for detail</u> and am able to work calmly under pressure. I use a variety of creative methods to ensure that the results of my work are effective. I am sensitive to the needs of the customer.

After I left school, I worked as an apprentice for a carpenter and attended classes at my local college, eventually gaining a diploma in furniture restoration. After four years, I took a job at a small antique shop where **b** <u>I gained valuable experience in restoring items from a range of eras</u>. I was also tasked with delivering lessons to interested customers on furniture repair.

c <u>I would very much welcome the opportunity to discuss this role with you</u> as **d** <u>I feel I could be a great asset to your café due to my passion and commitment</u> to restoring people's beloved furniture no matter how difficult it can be. Please feel free to contact me to arrange an interview.

Yours sincerely,

Valentina Ricci

2 Match sentences a–d in the email with purposes 1–4. Read the Focus box and check your answers.

1 Stress why you would be good for that position.
2 Adjectives to describe yourself that match the job description.
3 Ask for a chance to discuss the position in person.
4 Briefly describe your experience.

Matching your covering email to the advert

In order to write a good covering email, you need to do several things.
Choose words that match the job description to describe yourself.
I have an eye for detail.
I am fluent in English.
I have excellent communication skills.
Stress why you would be good for that job or position.
I believe I am the perfect fit for (your company) because …
I feel I would be a great asset to (your company) because …
Briefly mention your relevant experience and what you have learned.
As a student, I worked part-time for/at … where I demonstrated …
I gained valuable experience in … and was also tasked with …
More recently I worked for … where I became
expert at …
Ask for a chance to discuss the role in person (you are asking for an interview).
I would very much welcome the opportunity to discuss this role with you.
I would be happy to attend an interview at any time.

3 Put the words in the correct order to make sentences.

1 very / skills / have / active listening / I / strong

2 happy to / an interview / I would be / at any time / attend

3 a great asset / I feel / to your company / be / I would

4 a media company / more recently / worked for / I

5 I've worked as / where / monitoring social media / a social media manager / I was tasked with

6 the perfect fit / my brand knowledge / for your company / I believe I am / because of

4 Match sentences 1–5 from the email with the job requirements listed in the advertisement.

1 I have a good eye for detail. _____
2 I am able to work calmly under pressure. _____
3 I use a variety of creative methods to ensure that the results of my work are effective. _____
4 I am also aware of the emotions connected to the furniture that I repair and am sensitive to the needs of the customer. _____
5 I have passion and a commitment to restoring people's beloved furniture no matter how difficult it can be. _____

5 Complete the second sentences with the words in the box so they mean the same as the first.

adapt   ideas   information   oriented
others   support

1 We need a good team worker.
   I enjoy sharing ideas with _____ .
2 We're looking for someone who's committed to innovation.
   I am always keen to think of new _____ .
3 This job requires an independent thinker.
   I am able to find solutions to problems without _____ from others.
4 You need to have effective communication skills.
   I try to use a variety of methods to share _____ with my colleagues.
5 You need to have a good eye for detail.
   I am detail-_____ .
6 We need someone who's flexible.
   I am always willing to _____ to a situation as needed.

Prepare

6 You're going to write an email applying for the job of Chief Listening Officer. Make notes of the skills you have that relate to the job description in the advert.

7 Decide what information you can write in each paragraph of your email and what phrases you can use.
  • Paragraph 1: Say why you're writing
  • Paragraph 2: Describe your skills
  • Paragraph 3: Describe your experience
  • Paragraph 4: Ask for a chance to discuss the role in person

Write

8 Write your application email.

Vocabulary
Money phrases

1 **Join words in box A with words in box B to make phrasal verbs. Then, match them with meanings 1–8.**

A	cut get live pay set splash stock take

B	aside back back on into debt on out out (on) up on

1 buy a lot of something in order to keep it for later use

2 keep something, especially money, so that it can be used for a specific purpose
....

3 give someone money that you owe them
....

4 reduce the amount of something
....

5 get money from your bank account
....

6 spend a lot of money on something
....

7 have a particular amount of money to buy food and other necessary things
....

8 start owing money
....

2 **Complete the sentences with one word.**
1 Dan just .... out over £25,000 on a new car.
2 Almost half our monthly salary .... on our mortgage every month.
3 Can we go to the bank? I need to .... out some cash.
4 I'm putting on weight. I need to .... back on all the cakes I buy!
5 I've only got £100 to .... on for the rest of the month.
6 Last year, I .... into debt and struggled to pay the money back.
7 My fridge has broken so I've had to .... up on tinned food.
8 We try to .... aside £200 a month for our summer holiday.

Grammar
Mistakes in the past

3 **Match sentences 1–7 with sentences a–g.**
1 I've got no money left this month. ....
2 My sister's not talking to me at the moment. ....
3 I missed my train earlier. ....
4 I shared a secret with a friend and she told everyone. ....
5 I left college after just one year. ....
6 I decided to stay home. ....
7 I've made a dentist's appointment for 8 a.m. on Saturday. ....

a I was supposed to arrive at 10 but got there at 11.
b I shouldn't have forgotten her birthday.
c I could have gone out but I didn't want to.
d I wish I'd stayed and finished my course.
e If only I hadn't spent it all on clothes.
f I wish I hadn't said anything to her.
g I should have made it for later!

4 **Choose the correct alternatives.**
1 Yesterday was a waste of time. We shouldn't *bother/have bothered* going.
2 Helen *was supposed to/wished she had* come round today but I haven't seen her.
3 You could *have/have had* more time if you'd needed it.
4 Jonny *should/shouldn't* have been rude to Beth. She was only trying to help.
5 We could *go/have gone* to the concert tonight but we're not going to.
6 You shouldn't *be/have been* so lazy. It won't help you get a job.
7 Oh no, it's raining again. I wish I'*d/hadn't* brought an umbrella.

5 **Complete the comments with the correct form of the verbs in the box.**

eat   forget   get   listen   pick up   say   spend   waste

@alexroanoke	3 hrs ago
I woke up ten minutes after the start of my job interview today. I wish I ¹ .... to set my alarm. What's your #regretoftheday?	

@marymary	2 hrs ago
I feel really fat. I wish I ² .... that second piece of cake.	

@steveo	2 hrs ago
I was supposed ³ .... on a plane to Rome today but instead I'm lying in bed with flu.	

@alibell	1 hr ago
I could ⁴ .... the day at the beach but for some reason I volunteered to work. Now I'm wondering why.	

@bettyb	1 hr ago
I wish I ⁵ .... my keys before closing my front door this morning. #lockedout	

@purplerain	45 minutes ago
I went outside without a coat and got soaked. I should ⁶ .... to my mum.	

@paulkent	30 minutes ago
I should ⁷ .... 'thank you' to the person who helped me pick up my shopping when it fell out of the bag but I was so stressed I forgot. #feelbad #regretoftheday.	

@littlesmithy	5 minutes ago
I should have finished a report for my boss by now. If only I ⁸ .... my afternoon on social media. 🙂	

Vocabulary
Crime (robbery)

1 Match the sentence halves.

1 The burglars researched and ____
2 They stole diamonds and then left ____
3 They evaded ____
4 Eventually, they were caught ____
5 They went on ____
6 They pleaded ____
7 The jury found them ____
8 They were sentenced ____

a arrest for six months.
b the scene of the crime.
c to five years in jail.
d not guilty.
e planned their robbery carefully.
f by the police.
g trial four months later.
h guilty of their crime.

2 Complete the article with the phrases in the box.

> broke into   charge him with
> evade arrest   plead guilty
> leaving the scene of the crime   planned
> sentenced to

A robbery gone wrong

There are plenty of videos of unsuccessful burglars online. One perfect example is of a man who ¹____ a store one night, falling through the ceiling. He clearly hadn't ²____ the raid very carefully because when he tried to leave via the front door he couldn't get out. He tried to exit through the hole in the ceiling but fell back down again. Realising that he wasn't able to ³____ by ⁴____ , he sat down calmly and waited for the police to arrive and ⁵____ robbery. With the CCTV video evidence, he sensibly decided to ⁶____ and was later ⁷____ three years in prison.

Grammar
Quantifiers

3 Choose the correct alternatives.

1 Some of us *is/are* going to the Chinese restaurant later.
2 Each of my brothers *is/are* very outgoing.
3 Every *person/people* in my class wished me a happy birthday.
4 We've been here a couple of *time/times* before.
5 No cars *was/were* allowed on the roads during the carnival.
6 We don't have *much/many* coffee left.
7 We should take both *key/keys* in case we come home separately.
8 Can either of you *lend/lends* me £5?

4 Correct the mistakes in five of the sentences.

1 I woke up several time during the night last night.
2 Are there any biscuits in the cupboard?
3 There are loads of people in town today.
4 I only have little time before I have to go to a meeting.
5 No people has ever said that to me before!
6 Both Jack and Jemma are on holiday today.
7 There are plenty of food for everyone.
8 Neither of the six children looked happy.

5 Complete the article with the words in the box.

> all   both   every   a few   few   neither   none   several

The day the Mona Lisa became famous

The theft of the Mona Lisa in 1911 was significant for one main reason. It made the painting famous. Prior to the theft, ¹____ people outside the art world had heard of it. After the theft, ²____ major newspaper around the world carried the story. People even flocked to the gallery to look at the empty space where it had hung.

The theft was carried out by a group of three Italians. As the museum was closing, ³____ three of the men hid in a cupboard in the gallery. After the staff had left, they took the painting out of its frame and out of the museum. ⁴____ of the Louvre staff noticed. The theft was discovered by a visiting artist ⁵____ hours later.

The police spent weeks searching for the missing work of art. They even questioned ⁶____ famous people. ⁷____ American tycoon JP Morgan and artist Pablo Picasso were interviewed. ⁸____ of them were involved. Eventually, 28 months after taking the painting, one of the thieves tried to sell it. The dealer was suspicious and contacted the police. The man was arrested and sentenced to eight months in jail.

5c

Vocabulary
Money

1 **Reorder the letters to make words that match the definitions.**

1. Money that a bank charges when you borrow money   *tenetsri*
2. A bad economic situation in a country   *cosineres*
3. Things you buy in order to make money   *mensestintv*
4. Money you have in the bank for a (long) period of time   *vngisas*
5. Money you receive when you are retired   *nineops*
6. Money you receive regularly through work or investments   *coniem*
7. Something that is cheaper than normal   *abaring*
8. Money you give to an organisation to help it   *notdanoi*
9. The general increase in prices   *anionlift*
10. The amount of money you have available to spend   *dtegbu*

2 **Complete the conversations with the words in the box.**

> bargains   budget   donation   inflation
> income   interest   investment
> pension   recession   savings

1. **A:** I need a new bank account. I only get 1 percent ¹ _____ at this bank.
   B: You should try a ² _____ account at my bank. They offer 2.5 percent.
2. **A:** My monthly ³ _____ hasn't gone up at all since I retired.
   B: Well, that's because the economy is in a deep ⁴ _____ .
   A: I know, but ⁵ _____ means that prices have gone up but what I get has stayed the same. So technically, my ⁶ _____ has actually gone down.
3. **A:** I'd like to make a ⁷ _____ to a charity every month but I'm not sure which one.
   B: What's your ⁸ _____ ?
   A: £10 a month.
   B: You should choose a small charity where your money can make a real difference.
4. **A:** I'm thinking of buying a flat with the money I inherited. There are some real ⁹ _____ in the east of the city.
   B: I think that's a great idea. It'd be a really good ¹⁰ _____ .

Language focus
Adverb + adjective collocations

3 **Which adjective doesn't usually go with the adverb?**

1. relatively   *new/qualified/simple/small*
2. deeply   *concerned/dangerous/personal/religious*
3. highly   *effective/successful/unlikely/wrong*
4. perfectly   *good/legal/normal/ridiculous*
5. widely   *available/disappointed/known/used*
6. absolutely   *easy/essential/right/true*

4 **Complete the conversations with the collocations in the box.**

> absolutely ridiculous   bitterly cold   completely different
> perfectly safe   relatively simple   widely available

1. **A:** Are you sure it's OK to drink the tap water here?
   B: Yes, don't worry. It's _____ .
2. **A:** Is this paint the same colour as the paint in the living room?
   B: No, it's not. It's _____ !
3. **A:** Apparently, we all have to attend training on how to use the accounts software.
   B: What? The same software we've been using for five years? That's _____ !
4. **A:** Do I need a scarf and hat?
   B: Absolutely. It's _____ out there.
5. **A:** Have you downloaded that computer game you told me about?
   B: No. Unfortunately, it's not _____ yet. You can only get it in a few regions.
6. **A:** You just press this button here and then pull the lever here.
   B: OK. Well, that seems _____ .

5 **Choose the best adverb a, b, c or d.**

> **The largest flower auction in the world**
>
> Aalsmeer Flower Auction is the largest flower auction in the world. Based in The Netherlands, it sits in the largest building by footprint in the world at 518,000 square metres. It's ¹ _____ possible to lose your way in this vast building and get ² _____ lost.
>
> The auction is ³ _____ used by companies that want to sell their flowers internationally, from common cut flowers to ⁴ _____ rare decorative plants. The flowers are moved around on vehicles at high speed. Visitors are allowed to buy tickets and watch, but they're required to stand on a special walkway which ensures they're ⁵ _____ safe.
>
> Some tourists confuse Aalsmeer with Keukenhof which is the world's biggest flower garden. However, it is ⁶ _____ different. At Keukenhof, they can see 7 million tulips and other flowers up close in spring. At Aalsmeer, they can simply watch the logistics of an auction in action.

1	a absolutely	b relatively	c entirely	d highly
2	a deeply	b bitterly	c widely	d totally
3	a completely	b entirely	c highly	d widely
4	a widely	b deeply	c relatively	d highly
5	a deeply	b highly	c perfectly	d widely
6	a bitterly	b perfectly	c entirely	d highly

Vocabulary
Phrases with *leave*

1 Complete the sentences with one word. The first letter is given to help you.

1 I'm really sorry. I put my mug on the table and it's left a **m**_____ .

2 For goodness sake, leave me **a**_____ . I don't want to talk to you!

3 I need to go home. I think I left the iron **o**_____ .

4 Why do you always leave the bathroom in such a **m**_____? Please tidy it up!

5 The garage left a **m**_____ on our home phone. Your car's ready.

6 My hands are freezing. I stupidly left my gloves at **h**_____ .

7 I'm not surprised you can't find your glasses. You always leave them lying **a**_____ .

8 Anna wants a birthday surprise? Leave it to **m**_____ . I'll think of something.

English in action
Deal with and resolve conflicts

2 Match sentences 1–4 with uses a–d.

1 I'm only asking. _____

2 It was my fault. I apologise. _____

3 Don't worry. It's nothing. _____

4 Don't blame me. _____

a Accepting responsibility and apologising

b Responding to an apology

c Denying responsibility

d Responding to denial

3 Put the words in the correct order to makes sentences and questions. Then match them with uses a–d in Exercise 2.

1 deal / it's / big / no

_____

2 nothing / I / with / had / it / do / to

_____

3 sort / promise / out, / I / I'll / it

_____

4 do / again / try / to / it / not

_____

5 me / nothing / do / it's / to / with / got

_____

6 should / careful / I / more / been / have

_____

7 did / then / well, / who ?

_____

8 sorry, / I / spill / I'm / did / drink / so / your ?

_____

4 Complete the conversations with one word.

1 **A:** Who left that old food in the fridge? The whole office stinks!
   B: I have to [1]_____ up. It's mine.
   A: Oh well, it's no big [2]_____ really.
   B: You're right, it does smell awful. I'll [3]_____ it out now.

2 **A:** Why isn't Jack at this meeting?
   B: It's entirely my [4]_____ . I forgot to let him know it was happening.
   A: Don't worry. We can get him on the conference phone.

3 **A:** Did you leave these dirty footprints all over the house?
   B: Don't [5]_____ me.
   A: Well, who did it [6]_____ ?
   B: I guess it was Jon.

5 Complete the conversation using the prompts.

Manager: OK, so you're annoyed because Andy takes the lead in all our projects and I'm frustrated because you and Andy don't get on.

Employee: That's right.

Manager: [1]_____
(let's/try/find/solution), shall we?

Employee: OK. [2]_____
(What/about/Andy and I) work on different projects?

Manager: [3]_____
(don't think/going/work). You both have different skill sets which I need on all our projects.

Employee: [4]_____
(understand). Unfortunately, I can't see another way of solving the issue.

Manager: [5]_____
(why/don't/see/I) can give you the leadership role on some projects and Andy the leadership role on others?

Employee: [6]_____
(sound/reasonable)

Manager: [7]_____
(make/sense/because) then you both get a chance to develop your management skills but you'll both be clear about who makes the final decisions.

Employee: OK, that sounds great to me. I just hope that Andy agrees, too.

5

Reading

1 Read the article. Which topic does the writer mainly focus on?
- the cost of items
- the location of items in the store
- the packaging of items
- the behaviour of customers
- the motivation of store owners

2 Read the article again. Match paragraphs 1–6 in the article with topics a–f.

a We get more but each item doesn't necessarily cost less. ......

b We all need to notice the price and weight of items. ......

c We buy double the amount that we wanted. ......

d We think we're getting the top deal but it's not always true. ......

e We're all fooled by the actions of stores. ......

f We pay less but might actually get less for our money. ......

3 Answer the questions with between one and four words in the article.

1 What discount does a store actually offer with *buy one, get one free* deals?

2 According to the writer, what is free with a *buy one, get one free* deal?

3 What price should shoppers pay attention to when buying chocolate bars?

4 What does the writer say shoppers are highly unlikely to do when bulk buying?

5 Why might a product at €2.50 be better than the same one at €2.00?

6 According to the writer, what do stores depend on shoppers being unable to do?

7 According to research, what might the problem be with a *The lowest ever price* deal?

8 According to the writer, what will paying attention to product prices and weights help us to do?

4 Find the words in the box in the article. Then match them with definitions 1–10.

bulk-buy economical evaluate forced
a good deal hard-earned labelled multi-pack
push up trick

1 increase ......
2 judge how good something is ......
3 a package containing more than one item of a product ......
4 an arrangement where both buyer and seller benefit ......
5 attached with a piece of paper that gives information ......
6 using money carefully without wasting any ......
7 something that makes you believe something that's not true ......
8 made someone do something they don't want to do ......
9 purchase something in large amounts, usually at a lower price ......
10 achieved after a lot of work and effort ......

5 Complete the sentences with words in the article.

1 My mother is a very careful shopper. She ...... recognises a good deal when she sees one.

2 Pay ...... attention to the labels. They tell you how much salt and sugar are in the food.

3 I can't believe I ...... for such a silly trick. Never again!

4 The supermarket's selling both walnut and olive bread for just £1 a loaf. On ...... of that, it's freshly made in the store so it's still warm.

5 I spent twice as ...... as I wanted to in the shop but I only seem to have bought two extra things!

6 Tick the sentences that you think the writer would agree with.

1 Shoppers should take advantage of deals whenever they are on offer.
2 Most deals are designed to trick shoppers out of their hard-earned money.
3 Shoppers should be careful not to buy more than they want or need.
4 Stores understand that we don't want to waste time evaluating deals.
5 Shopping online is the best way to find deals and compare prices.

The tricks stores use to get us to spend more money

1 We've all gone into a shop and spent far more than we wanted. We have three things on our list but come out with ten. We shouldn't feel too guilty about this though, as shop owners employ various psychological tricks to make us part with our hard-earned cash. Remember – you're not the only one falling for these tricks.

2 Take **buy one get one free** deals. We think we're getting 100 percent free but what the store is actually offering us is a 50 percent discount on two products. That's the same thing, you might say, but really, it's not. You wanted one item but the offer forced you to buy two, meaning you spent twice as much and nothing was free at all. There's also the issue of exactly what price is discounted. Stores have been known to push up the price of the item on sale so that your discount is reduced.

3 Another trick is to offer what seems to be good deals when you bulk-buy. For example, €2.77 for a pack of seven chocolate bars seems better than €1.50 for a pack of four. However, it's the price per item that's important here. It's more economical to get the smaller bundle at 38 cents as opposed to 40 cents per bar. On other occasions, the cost per bar may be the same whether you buy a four-pack or a nine-pack. Either way, if you buy the multi-pack, you've spent more than you needed to. Of course, how many of us are going to calculate and compare prices in this way? Stores know that we have better things to do with our time.

4 Weight is another factor. Shoppers don't necessarily pay close attention to how much of a product they receive for what price. That means they might not make the best decision about which item to buy, choosing an item 'on sale' at €2.00 because it seems cheaper than a similar product for sale at €2.50. However, the €2.50 product might be in a bigger box which means you actually get more for your money. On top of that, some manufacturers have been known to give the weight of one size of a product in grams and another in kilograms so that it's difficult for customers to compare. The bigger packet may seem like a more economical option, but in fact two smaller packets work out cheaper.

5 All in all, it's our inability to remember prices of items that stores rely on. Because of this, we're unable to truly recognise what is a real bargain and what is a trick. Prices may be labelled as **The lowest ever price** but often it hasn't changed for weeks, so we're not actually going to pay any less. There's been research which suggests the price is occasionally higher than it was in the past, too.

6 So, what does this mean for the shopper? It means that we need to pay more attention to the price of products we regularly buy and how much we get for that money. That way, we're better able to evaluate a deal. We can do a quick calculation to see whether an offer is in fact a bargain or simply a trick to get us to spend more.

Listening

1 🔊 **5.01** **Listen to a talk. Why does the speaker start with an anecdote about China?**

  a To explain the reasons behind something.

  b To engage the audience and introduce the topic.

  c To argue a point of view.

2 **Listen again. Complete the notes with one or two words from the talk in each gap.**

A cashless society

Pros

It'd save people and businesses ¹_____.

Easier to buy things ²_____.

Significantly fewer ³_____.

Cons

No access to money if technology ⁴_____.

People without ⁵_____ or ⁶_____ ability will struggle.

⁷_____ could steal all your money.

What is needed for a cashless society?

• An online ⁸_____ that works and is secure.

• Support so that no one in society is left ⁹_____.

---

3 **Match topics 1–5 with reasons why they were mentioned a–e. Then listen and check.**

  1 President of the US _____

  2 Sweden _____

  3 Mobile phone battery _____

  4 Debt _____

  5 Governments _____

  a An example of technology failing to work

  b The extreme reaction of a shop assistant to a customer

  c The need to ensure everyone has access to a bank account

  d An example of the use of advanced payment technology

  e The result for people who are bad at money management

Writing

1 **Quickly read the description and choose the best title.**

  a A new job

  b First impressions

  c A friendly colleague

The first time I saw Leon was in 2007. I'd got a new job and he was the first person I noticed when I walked into the office. He was in his mid-20s like me. He had short hair which was straight and as dark as the night sky. His hairline was quite high and I wondered then if his hair was receding. It was.

He had a really symmetrical face. I think that's what attracted me to him and I kept losing myself in his dark brown eyes which seemed as deep as the ocean. His nose was elegant and he had full lips. He had a fair complexion with stubble around his chin.

I asked him where I could find a notebook and he offered to give me one of his. His voice was rich and soft like velvet. It was a voice I thought I could listen to all day. When he stood up to get the notebook, I saw that he was above average height. He was solidly-built with broad shoulders and he looked as strong as an ox.

He seemed to be shy, but I know now that it was only with me. With others he was confident but he seemed happy to let me do the talking. On the odd occasion that he smiled, his face lit up and his cheeks revealed dimples. He seemed to be made up of many layers and I wanted to know what they were.

He talked about the company as though he'd been there for years. He'd only just started, however, so was almost as new as I was. This was the thing in common that kept us talking day after day, sharing our experiences. It wasn't long before he was my best friend, although it took a little longer for him to become my husband.

2 Read the description. What adjectives are used to describe Leon's ...

1 hair? ....
2 face? ....
3 eyes? ....
4 nose? ....
5 mouth? ....
6 build? ....
7 voice? ....
8 character? ....

3 Match the words in the box with features 1–8 in Exercise 2. Some words can be used twice.

bald freckles high-pitched muscular prominent
stubble thick thin wide

Using similes

A simile is a comparison between two people, things or actions. The words *like* or *as* will normally be used in the comparison.

*His legs were **like sticks**, they were so thin.*
*She walked **as if she was carrying a stack of books on top of her head**.*

Similes are useful for making character descriptions more engaging and memorable. They allow the writer to describe more than appearance and action. With similes, the writer can give a strong impression of how he or she felt about the person.

*She was **like a breath of fresh air in a really stuffy office**.*

Some common similes are:

as blind as a bat
as dry as a bone
as dull as dishwater
as good as gold
as light as a feather
as quiet as a mouse
as sick as a parrot
like two peas in a pod

4 Find four examples of similes in the description in Exercise 1.

1 ....
2 ....
3 ....
4 ....

5 Match the sentence halves.

1 His eyes were as dark as ....
2 Her hair was red, like ....
3 Her smile lit up the room as if ....
4 His anger was sudden, as if ....
5 Her glasses were thick like ....
6 He was as quiet as ....
7 When he talked, the corner of his mouth turned up as if ....
8 Her voice was loud like ....

a someone had turned on a bright light.
b the bottom of a glass bottle.
c the night.
d a foghorn.
e a ball of fire had burst out of him.
f he wanted to smile.
g the sky during a beautiful sunset.
h a mouse.

Prepare

6 You're going to write a description of the first time you met someone you know. Make notes about:
- what you noticed about the person's appearance
- what you noticed about the person's character
- the person's actions/behaviour

7 Write a list of words and at least four possible similes that you can use to describe the person's appearance, character and behaviour.

Write

8 Write your description. Include some of the words and similes on your list in Exercise 7.

Vocabulary

Common idioms

1 Match the words in box A with the words in box B to make idioms.

A	be a be out of be over be a piece cost an arm drive me take my

B	and a leg breath away of cake pain the moon this world up the wall

2 Choose the correct alternatives.

1 This cake is out of this *Earth/world*.
2 This view takes my *breath/air* away.
3 I hope Mariah likes this ring. It cost an arm and a *foot/leg*!
4 That noise is driving me up the *road/wall*.
5 The homework won't take you long. It's a piece of *cake/bread*.
6 People assume things because of my taste in fashion but you can't judge a book by its *cover/title*.
7 I got the job! I'm over the *moon/sky*.
8 I have to walk 20 minutes to the nearest bus stop. It's *an ache/a pain*.

3 Complete the sentences with idioms.

1 My baby daughter's smile ....
   (is extremely beautiful)
2 Greg's constant chatter ....
   (makes me angry)
3 Just because she likes to dress differently means nothing. You can't ....
   (decide what someone is like based on appearance)
4 The flight to Paris last week ....
   (was very expensive)
5 Luke got top marks in all his exams. We're all ....
   (really happy)
6 I have to get up at 5 a.m. to get to work on time. It's such ....
   (annoying)
7 The washing machine looks difficult to use but it's actually .... ,
   (very easy)
8 This coffee is ....
   (like nothing I've tasted before)

Grammar

Verb + *-ing* and infinitive with *to*

4 Choose the correct alternatives.

1 There's no point *to go/going* to the bank now. It'll be closed.
2 It's best *to go/going* for a run first thing so you get it out of the way.
3 I can't imagine *to live/living* anywhere else except here.
4 We stopped *to get/getting* some lunch about an hour into our walk.
5 I really regret not *to tell/telling* you about this sooner.
6 Dan managed *to buy/buying* his first car after nine months of saving.
7 I don't remember *to lock/locking* the door. Did you see me doing it?
8 *To have/Having* a lie-in is one of the biggest pleasures in life.

5 Make sentences using the prompts and the correct form of the verbs.

1 We / consider / get / a dog last year.
2 It / not / worth / cry / over a broken dish.
3 It's easy / get / around the city on foot.
4 Megan / keep / send / me really funny gifs.
5 you / remember / meet / me for the first time?
6 I / can't wait / have / a lovely, relaxing bath tonight.
7 It was good of you / come / round and help yesterday.
8 Dom / message / this morning / invite / me for dinner.

6 Complete the comments with the correct form of the verbs in the box.

complain   eat   have (x3)   laugh   moan   play   watch

The things we love to hate

I love watching TV but I think reality TV shows are awful. Most of the time they're full of shallow people being unkind to each other. I usually avoid **1**................................ them, but when I do come across one, I quite enjoy **2**................................ at those awful people.

Debbie, Tyneside

My mum used to cook Brussels sprouts for us when we were kids even though we all hated **3**................................ them. When she cooks them for us today, we still complain about **4**................................ them on our plates, but it's more of a ritual than an actual dislike. It's nice **5**................................ something to connect us.

Marcella, London

6................................ in a band myself, I get really annoyed at singers who become famous without **7**................................ much talent. There's no point **8**................................ about them because they'll always exist, but I can't help **9**................................ anyway!

Hugo, Devon

Vocabulary
Negotiating

1 Complete the sentences with one word in each gap. The first letter is given to help you.

1 Marc and I **f**_____**o**_____ over something silly and now we're not speaking.

2 I always try to avoid **c**_____ . I prefer it when everyone agrees.

3 It's hard to **s**_____ **c**_____ when someone's shouting at you.

4 I have a strong **b**_____ with all my siblings. We've always been close.

5 There seems to be a lot of **t**_____ in the office today. Why is everyone stressed?

6 The first thing a good salesperson does is **b**_____ **t**_____ with the customer.

7 Stop **i**_____ me and let me speak!

8 Anyone who's worked hard at something deserves **p**_____ .

2 Choose the correct option a, b or c.

How to be a good salesperson
I've been in sales for over 30 years. Here are my top tips for getting and keeping long-term customers.

- Ask the customer questions to find out what they want. This will help to create a positive **¹**_____ between the two of you.

- Avoid **²**_____ the customer. Let them speak, listen carefully and then tell them how you can help them.

- Pay attention to the customer's body language. If you notice any **³**_____ , suggest speaking again on a different day.

- **⁴**_____ calm, even if the customer tells you they're not interested in your product. Leave them to think about it and follow up in a few days.

- Avoid future conflict by being honest about any issues that might arise later and plan ways to overcome them. This will help to **⁵**_____ trust between you. Of course, never **⁶**_____ the product but be open to discussing its weaknesses if necessary.

- Once the customer has received the product, talk to them to find out how they're getting on with it. **⁷**_____ with them if they have any problems that need solving.

	a		b		c
1	a preference		b link		c bond
2	a interrupting		b preventing		c participating
3	a threats		b tension		c pressure
4	a Stay		b Stand		c Have
5	a make		b build		c construct
6	a criticise		b blame		c praise
7	a Share		b Partner		c Cooperate

Grammar
Reported speech

3 Correct the mistakes in the reported speech.

1 'I've been living here for six years.'
She told me that she'd lived there for six years.

2 'I'll meet you here at 6 p.m. tomorrow.'
He said that he'll meet us there at 6 p.m. the next day.

3 'Do you want to get a pizza?'
She asked me if I want to get a pizza.

4 'We can go in my car.'
She said we would go in her car.

5 'Where's the match taking place?'
He asked me where was the match taking place.

6 'Please be quiet.'
He asked us be quiet.

4 Read conversations A and B. Then complete conversation C.

A

Georgina: I'm worried about my brother Josh. He can't find a job and he's feeling depressed about it.

Kate: Don't worry. I'm sure he'll find something soon.

Georgina: Are there are any jobs where you work?

Kate: I doubt it. Do you fancy meeting up sometime soon? I fancy a night out.

Georgina: Sounds good.

B

Georgina: My brother Josh has moved to Manchester.

Becky: Has he? Why?

Georgina: He's got a job there. I can't remember his job title but it involves manufacturing. We're all really pleased but I miss him.

Becky: I bet.

Georgina: Anyway, what night are you and Kate free next week? I'd love to have you round for dinner.

C

Becky: I saw Georgina last week. She told me that her brother, Josh **¹**_____ to Manchester because he **²**_____ a new job there.

Kate: Oh, good. Doing what?

Becky: She said it **³**_____ manufacturing.

Kate: I'm pleased for him. I saw her last month and she said that he **⁴**_____ fed up because he couldn't find work. I told her **⁵**_____ worry and I was right. She asked me if I **⁶**_____ of any jobs going where I work.

Becky: Ha! Hardly! Anyway, when I saw her, she asked me what night we **⁷**_____ free next week. She wants to invite us round for dinner. She said she **⁸**_____ Josh so I think she wants some company.

Kate: Sounds good to me. I'm free anytime.

Vocabulary

Reporting verbs

1 Choose the correct alternatives.

1 I'd forgotten about my dentist's appointment. Thanks for *remembering*/*reminding* me.

2 My maths teacher *accused*/*threatened* to tell my parents if I didn't behave.

3 My youngest daughter *denied*/*admitted* drawing on the wall, but I knew it was her.

4 I wanted to turn round and go home but Mike *agreed*/*insisted* we keep going.

5 My son *agrees*/*refuses* to keep his room tidy despite constant nagging!

6 I wasn't sure about joining a gym but Sara *advised*/*convinced* me it was a good idea.

7 Beatriz *apologised*/*admitted* for dropping food on her friend's sofa.

8 My brother always *blames*/*denies* me for his broken bike but it wasn't me!

2 Complete the conversations with the correct form of the words in the boxes.

1 | accuse   convince   deny   insist |

A: Jamie has just **1**............... me of trying to steal his idea and present it as my own but I'd honestly thought of it myself.

B: Did you **2**............... stealing it?

A: Of course I did, because he's wrong – but he doesn't believe me.

B: Did you **3**............... that you were telling the truth?

A: I did, but nothing I said could **4**............... him.

2 | advise   blame   refuse   threaten |

A: My boss just asked me to work overtime at the weekend. I **5**............... .

B: What did he say?

A: He **6**............... to sack me if I didn't do it but I **7**............... him not to do that as I'd complain to his manager if he tried it.

B: What did he say to that?

A: He **8**............... me for the poor sales in our department.

3 | admit   agree   apologise   remind |

A: I finally talked to Alison yesterday after our argument. I **9**............... her that it's Dad's birthday next week. She **10**............... to come to his party.

B: Oh, that's good. Did you **11**............... for what you said?

A: Yeah, I said I was sorry for not trying to understand her side of things. She **12**............... that she'd been wrong, too.

B: Sounds like you can be friends again then. Or cousins!

Language focus

Verb patterns after reporting verbs

3 Choose the correct alternatives.

1 I denied *breaking*/*to break* the toaster even though it was me who did it.

2 My landlord has finally agreed *letting*/*to let* me have a cat.

3 My neighbour wrongly accused me of *playing*/*to play* loud music.

4 My lawyer advised me *paying*/*to pay* the parking fine without argument.

5 Dad refuses *to increase*/*us to increase* our pocket money, even though we beg!

6 I always insist *to take*/*on taking* my shoes off before entering someone's home.

7 Our teacher has just reminded *to get*/*us to get* our assignment in.

8 I've just convinced my boss *about to give*/*to give* me a pay rise!

4 Make sentences using the prompts. Then add them to conversations 1–6.

a David's / threatened / cancel / the party

b I / admit / have / one or two

c I've / agreed / help / a friend move house

d Norah / insisted / pay / it

e Remind / me / never / ask / you for advice

f She / accused / me / borrow / her clothes

1 **A:** Shall we get the bill?
   B: ...... before she left.
   A: That was kind of her. I'll get it next time.

2 **A:** Why are you and Dani fighting?
   B: ...... when I didn't.
   A: Oh, that was me – I should have told her. Sorry!

3 **A:** Do you want to go see a film tomorrow?
   B: No, sorry. ....
   A: Maybe the next day then?

4 **A:** Have you eaten all the biscuits?
   B: No! ...... but that's all!
   A: There must be some left in the drawer then.

5 **A:** Did you do what I suggested?
   B: Yes. ...... again!
   A: Oh, didn't it work? What happened?

6 **A:** Why are you doing housework on a Friday night?
   B: Because ...... if I don't!
   A: Well, you do leave your clothes all over the house!

Listening

1 🔊 **6.01 Listen to two podcasts both dealing with a similar topic. What is that topic?**

a how to negotiate
b how to save money
c how to deal with conflict

2 Listen again. Which podcast discusses these things, 1, 2 or both (B)?

1 Start with some polite chat. ____
2 Do some research before you have your discussions. ____
3 Collect proof so that you can be persuasive. ____
4 Don't speak about money too soon. ____
5 Don't be afraid to state an amount which may seem silly. ____
6 Go to other companies so that you can be more persuasive. ____
7 Don't just consider money as a factor. ____
8 Make an excuse to leave the discussion if necessary. ____
9 Don't rush to make a decision. ____
10 End the conversation in a positive way. ____

3 Listen to podcast 1 again and complete the sentences.

1 The presenter's colleague received a higher salary because she'd _____ it.
2 The presenter suggests finding out about the company's _____ before discussions.
3 Research suggests that money is not the only reason for _____ .
4 The presenter recommends being _____ and _____ during discussions.
5 The presenter says that the discussions may end with a _____ offer from the company.
6 The presenter suggests ending the conversation by thanking the manager for _____ .

4 Listen to podcast 2 again and choose the best option, a or b.

1 The presenters agree that the process of buying a car is
   a hard to understand.
   b difficult to deal with.

2 Lara suggests that Mike starts the conversation with small talk to
   a build a connection with the salesperson.
   b put the salesperson at ease.

3 Lara says to avoid asking the salesperson
   a what his/her lowest price is.
   b for extras in the deal.

4 Lara says that salespeople expect customers to make an offer
   a at a ridiculously cheap price.
   b just below the asking price.

5 Lara suggests asking for extras
   a early in the process.
   b late in the process.

6 Lara says that it's a good idea to leave the negotiation so that
   a you can talk the offer through with someone else.
   b you can see if there are better offers elsewhere.

5 Match the words in bold with meanings a–f.

1 They offered me just a bit over my **existing** salary. ____
2 Are their **profits** increasing or decreasing? ____
3 Speak in a calm and friendly **manner**. ____
4 The situation could get **awkward**, but my sister-in-law is amazing at this kind of thing. ____
5 No doubt some of our listeners will **appreciate** them, too. ____
6 Make sure the salesperson hasn't included it in the **overall** price. ____

a understand how useful something is
b the way something is done
c including everything
d present
e money received by doing business
f making you feel embarrassed

6 Which podcast do you think these tips belong to, 1, 2 or both (B)?

1 Get them to throw in something for free. ____
2 Get the timing right. ____
3 Explain the purpose of your meeting beforehand. ____

Reading

1 **Read the forum quickly. What do you think a guilty pleasure is?**
 a Something you love to hate
 b Something you do that no one else does
 c Something you enjoy but feel bad about

2 **Read the article again. Which writer(s) (a–p) …**
 1 tries to find out about people by looking at their pictures? ....
 2 admits having unusual taste in music? ....
 3 like to correct someone? ....
 4 knows someone who got into trouble for something? ....
 5 avoids sharing something with others? ....
 6 feels bad about wasting something? ....
 7 use items that belong to their children? ....
 8 describe a day where they lazed around at home? ....

3 **Read the article again. Are the sentences true (T) or false (F)?**
 1 Brittany is fine about having so many guilty pleasures in one day. ....
 2 Markus says that Brittany's exact day is perfect for him. ....
 3 Chris thinks there's nothing wrong with his habit. ....
 4 Rik makes excuses to himself about his behaviour. ....
 5 Andrew enjoys the action he describes. ....
 6 Nick admits that he takes too many photos of himself. ....
 7 Bradley feels that he deserved a break. ....
 8 Certain films remind Fran of her daughter's childhood. ....

What are your guilty pleasures?

a Brittany
I've just spent all afternoon watching a box set while still wearing my pyjamas. I've had three cups of tea and eaten an entire week's worth of biscuits and later, I'm going to order a takeaway because I can't be bothered to cook. That's a lot of guilty pleasures in one day but I just don't care. What guilty pleasures do you enjoy?

b Markus
Your afternoon sounds great. Add in falling asleep in front of the TV and it'd be absolutely perfect!

c Geo
Our problem with ordering a takeaway is that we order enough for a small army and then either stuff our faces with it until we feel sick, or we throw some away. First the pleasure, then the guilt.

d Chris
I have a habit of eating that well-known hazelnut spread out of the jar with a teaspoon. I know I shouldn't but I just can't seem to help myself.

e Doug
My flatmate hates it when I do that so I've started using a dessert spoon just to irritate him. I make sure I get every last bit out of the jar, too. Don't want to miss out on any little bit.

f Kat
I put it on top of ice cream. One spoonful is enough but it's the tastiest thing ever.

g Rik
I secretly bring chocolate into the house so no one knows I have it. Then, I find a quiet corner and eat the whole lot. I don't feel bad about it. I tell myself that I'm saving my family from unnecessary calories.

h Andrew
Looking through people's photos online is definitely something I do and feel guilty about. I'm not really sure it's a pleasure, though. More like a depressing habit I've started and can't break.

i Nick
Taking a hundred selfies to find one good one must be the guilty pleasure of an entire generation, or so I've heard.

j Samera
I'm not sure this is much fun either.

4 Find phrases 1–6 in the article. Then choose the best definition a–b.

1 stuff (your) face
   a fill yourself with food   b talk about food
2 break a habit
   a start a habit   b stop a habit
3 chill out
   a take a nap   b relax
4 prove someone wrong
   a argue that someone is incorrect
   b find evidence that someone is incorrect
5 keep (your) feet on the ground
   a keep someone's attitude to life sensible
   b keep someone's intelligence high
6 catch sight of (someone)
   a see someone for a moment   b fail to see someone

5 Complete the sentences with the correct form of the phrases in Exercise 4.

1 Did I just _____ Jess across the street? It looked like her.
2 I told you it was down that road and not this one. I love _____ !
3 I've been biting my nails since I was a child so I'm unlikely to _____ in my 40s.
4 Just go home, take a bath and _____ .
5 I really _____ last night. I still feel sick today.
6 We all need someone to _____ so we don't get too arrogant.

---

k Paul

My wife insists she's right about pretty much everything, so when I prove her wrong, I make sure I fully enjoy it. Don't get me wrong, I love her very much but it's good to keep her feet on the ground every now and then.

l Silvie

Ha ha! I was drinking some tea when I read this and it came out my nose! In my case, it's my brother who I like to prove wrong.

m Bradley

I recently called in sick at work even though I wasn't. I'm not proud of it, but I felt I was owed it with all the extra hours I do and the fact that I'm rarely actually sick. I just chilled out at home reading, eating and sleeping while the kids were at school. Bliss.

n Lilia

My friend took a day off sick and went to a cricket match. He appeared on TV, the boss's wife caught sight of him and he lost his job! I have a few guilty pleasures as a parent. One is eating chocolate and sweets from the kids' sweetie drawer. Another is pretending I think computer games are bad but then I play their games when they're in bed.

o Fran

I watch my daughter's Disney films even when she's at play school and I'm alone in the house. They're strangely comforting. I guess they remind me of when I was a child and life was simpler and less confusing.

p Mynameismybusiness

Listening to Trevor Doonican's Greatest Hits from the 1960s. I know what you think – that I'm an elderly woman – but I'm actually a 31-year-old male. It reminds me of my grandma, OK?!

Writing

1 Read the emails and complete the sentences.

1 Darren is complaining about a _____ stay.
He wants a _____ .

2 Audrey is complaining about an
_____ . She wants a
_____ or her money back.

2 Match sentences a–g in the emails with purposes 1–4. Then read the Focus box and check your answers.

1 State the purpose for writing _____ _____

2 State what you want to happen _____ _____

3 Persuade the writer to agree with you _____

4 Make it clear that you expect a reply soon _____ _____

Using comment adverbs

Comment adverbs show how the writer feels about an event or situation. They refer to the whole clause or sentence. These adverbs commonly occur at the beginning of a clause or sentence, particularly in written English, although they can also occur before the verb or sometimes at the end of a sentence. When they occur at the beginning of a sentence, they are followed by a comma.
Here are examples of comment adverbs.

- to express hope, luck or (un)happiness
  Unfortunately, the only room available was a double.
  Hopefully, you will agree that this is a fair request.
- to express surprise or lack of surprise
  Clearly, your hotel failed to live up to its expectations.
  Obviously, I am disappointed with this situation.
- other common comment adverbs
  Apparently, this is a common problem.
  Frankly, I am unsure how anyone can sleep in that room.

● ● ●

Dear Sir/Madam,

ᵃI am writing to you regarding my stay at your hotel on 17th May. While I've stayed at your property on many occasions and been perfectly satisfied, on this occasion I was not.

Firstly, I'd booked a king-size bed but unfortunately, the only room available was a double. The room itself was adequate but the location was not. It was next to the lift which meant that all I could hear all night was machinery followed by people entering and exiting the floor. Frankly, I am unsure how anyone can sleep in that room.

The next morning, when I tried to enter the breakfast room, I was told that it was full and to come back later. As I had a meeting an hour later, I was unable to return and therefore did not eat. Clearly, ᵇyour hotel failed to live up to my expectations during my stay and I therefore feel that I am entitled to at least a 50 percent refund.

ᶜI look forward to hearing from you at your earliest convenience.

Darren Walters

● ● ●

Dear Sir/Madam,

ᵈI am writing concerning the S-X458 electric toothbrush I recently bought.

I was told that this toothbrush came with a working battery charger for the toothbrush and that it would last for at least five years. However, three weeks after purchasing the product, the charger failed and no longer works. Apparently, this is a common problem.

Obviously, I am disappointed with this situation and ᵉwould like to request either a refund or a replacement product with a properly working charger.

ᶠHopefully, you agree that this is a fair request and ᵍI look forward to your prompt response.

Audrey Green

3 Put the words in the correct order to makes sentences. Then match them with purposes 1–4 in Exercise 2.

1 making a / for a / I / am / claim / refund / full

2 hear / earliest / I / to / convenience / from you / hope / at your

3 claim / please / this email / a / refund / accept / as / for a

4 to / writing / am / complain / I / your event / about

5 not / purpose / this product / fit / is / for

6 the product / warranty / believe / is / I / under / still

4 Find the adverbs in the box in the emails and answer the questions. Then, check your ideas in the Focus box.

clearly   frankly   hopefully   obviously   unfortunately

1 Which adverb expresses hope or luck?

2 Which adverbs express a lack of surprise?

3 Which adverb shows you are being honest?

4 Which adverb expresses a lack of hope or luck?

5 Look at the adverbs in the box. Do they express hope/luck, happiness/unhappiness, surprise/lack of surprise or something else?

astonishingly   luckily   naturally   predictably   reluctantly   sadly

6 Choose the correct alternatives.
1 I was really looking forward to the event. *Luckily/Sadly*, it did not meet my expectations.
2 I am 195 cm tall. The bed was a single. *Astonishingly/Predictably*, the bed was too small.
3 We heard that the band had cancelled the concert on our journey there. *Naturally/Reluctantly*, we were disappointed.
4 The machine became extremely hot and spat out boiling water. *Clearly/Luckily*, no one was hurt.
5 We did not want to move to a different room but *apparently/reluctantly*, we agreed.
6 We arrived to discover the hotel was closed due to flooding. *Astonishingly/Frankly*, no one had told us.

Prepare

7 You attended a one-day music festival which was disappointing. Think of reasons why it could have been disappointing.

8 Plan an email of complaint to the festival event company. Decide what information you will put into each paragraph.

9 Choose phrases and adverbs to use in your email.

Write

10 Write your email of complaint.

Vocabulary
Social issues

1 Complete the news reports. The first letter is given to help you.

1 Our s_____ of l_____ has increased over the last 20 years. We have more money, own more property and live more comfortably.

2 U_____ has reached a record low this month with more people in jobs than ever before.

3 H_____ has increased with over 100 people living on the streets across the city.

4 Police spent the night dealing with s_____ u_____ . People poured onto the street yesterday to show their disgust at how a crime victim from the area was treated in court.

2 Match the social issues in the box with statements 1–9. You can use the issues more than once.

> energy efficiency   healthcare   inequality
> life expectancy   living standards   poverty

1 The gap between rich and poor seems to be increasing. _____

2 The average is about 71.5 years old globally. _____

3 In my town, people have more money and nicer things than they used to. _____

4 We need to do whatever we can to avoid wasting electricity and fuel. _____

5 Women's salaries in the company are lower than men's on average. _____

6 It's time that we turned to greener solutions. _____

7 The cost of medicine is very expensive without insurance. _____

8 My family was very poor when we grew up and we sometimes struggled. _____

9 It's currently lower for men than it is for women but that may change. _____

Grammar
Real conditionals

3 Match the sentence halves.

1 When I see people living on the streets, _____
2 If you donate money to our charity, _____
3 Unless we provide more beds, _____
4 As long as we understand the problem, _____
5 Provided that someone wants help, _____
6 Assuming it's safe, clean and affordable, _____

a we can try to solve it.
b nothing will change.
c any flat can provide a good home for someone.
d we'll make sure it goes to someone in need.
e that charity can help them to find a home.
f I feel really bad.

4 Complete the conversations with one word.

1 **A:** Do you think we'll get to the theatre in time tonight?
   B: Yes, as _____ as we get on a bus by 6 p.m.

2 **A:** I'm off to the airport now.
   B: OK. Call me as _____ as your flight lands.

3 **A:** I don't understand why Tom shouted at me. I'm on his side!
   B: I know, but _____ people are angry, they often shout at the ones they love.

4 **A:** So, everything's still OK for our day out tomorrow, right?
   B: Yeah, _____ something happens between now and tomorrow, it's all fine.

5 **A:** _____ we can't get train tickets, will you drive?
   B: I guess so, but I'd rather not.

6 **A:** Is Alison still coming next weekend?
   B: She'll be here on Saturday _____ that she doesn't have to work.

5 Make sentences using the prompts. Add commas if necessary.

1 Unless / you / get the large size / the shirt / not / fit me.
_____

2 When / my dog / see / me / she / come / running every time!
_____

3 I / not / come with you / if / you / not / want me to.
_____

4 You / do / fine in the exams / as long as / you / revise.
_____

5 Provided that / Jack / do / his part of the report soon / we / finish / it by 3 p.m.
_____

6 My car / always / stop / working / when / I / need / it the most.
_____

Grammar

Future forms and degrees of probability

1 Put sentences a–e in the correct place in the diagram.

Very sure (+)

a I doubt it'll happen.
b It might happen.
c It definitely won't happen.
d It'll probably happen.
e It'll definitely happen.

1 ....
2 ....
3 ....
4 ....
5 ....

Very sure (−)

2 Complete the predictions about 2050 with one word.

1 I don't think robots .... do everything for us.
2 We'll .... have some kind of microchip in our heads. I'm sure of it.
3 I .... that much will change. It'll all be very similar to now.
4 Living standards around the world .... likely to be better than now.
5 Life probably .... be all that much different. Just technology will change.
6 It's .... that we'll all travel in self-driving cars but I'm not sure. We don't have that technology.
7 There definitely .... be flying cars like you see in sci-fi films. That's unrealistic.
8 It's .... that humans will die out because of AI. Or maybe I just want that to be true!

3 Complete the conversations with phrases a–h.

1 A: I don't think ...... tonight.
   B: Why not? Has she got better things to do?
2 A: You may well ...... at tennis. I've got a sore ankle.
   B: Excuses, excuses!
3 A: I think it's unlikely that ...... this week.
   B: That's a shame. I was hoping we could go shopping one afternoon.
4 A: ...... to go away for the weekend or not.
   B: That sounds great. Alone though?
5 A: Have you got to the end of that book I lent you yet?
   B: No, and I ...... for a while. It's really long.
6 A: There's a delivery man outside with flowers.
   B: Well, I doubt .... I don't know anyone who would send me flowers.
7 A: I probably .... I'm not feeling great.
   B: Oh no, sorry to hear that. Sounds like bath and a bed for you.
8 A: ...... going to visit Maria next week. Do you want to come?
   B: Yeah, that'd be great. I haven't seen her for ages.

a he'll bring them here
b beat me today
c won't come out tonight
d I'll get any time off
e we'll see Becky tonight
f We're planning on
g definitely won't finish it
h I'm wondering whether

Vocabulary

Collocations with *make, take, do* and *give*

4 Choose the correct alternatives.

1 We didn't win but we gave it our best *attempt/shot*.
2 My manager can't attend the meeting so I'm taking his *place/space*.
3 These instructions don't make any *clear/sense* at all.
4 Have we made a *money/profit* today? I hope so!
5 You've done a really good *job/work* with the garden.
6 Do we have to go out to the party? I could do *with/without* it.
7 Could you give me *an arm/a hand*? I can't do this on my own.
8 I don't usually take a *danger/risk* with money but this investment seems secure.

5 Complete the article with the phrases in the box.

doing a lot of research   do without   get a good deal
give it your best shot   give priority   make a profit
take charge   taking a risk

Tips for starting a new business

It's not easy to start your own business and, in fact, many small businesses fail in the first year. Any new business owner needs to understand that they're [1] .... and that nothing is certain. They're also unlikely to [2] .... in the first year, so need to live on savings.

It's not enough just to [3] .... Effort only gets you part of the way. Give yourself a greater chance at success by [4] .... to find out if people want your product and service and exactly what their needs are. Keep costs low by [5] .... with your landlord and suppliers. [6] .... to things you definitely need and [7] .... those things that are desirable but not essential. You can get them later. [8] .... of your marketing strategy and promote your business.

7c

Vocabulary

Personal and professional relationships

1 **Complete the crossword.**

Across

7 My brother's wife (6-2-3)
8 Someone who uses my services at work (6)
9 My sister's husband (7-2-3)

Down

1 The person who was my girlfriend (2-7)
2 Someone I work with in a higher position than me (6, 9)
3 Someone I know but not well (12)
4 Someone who studies with me (9)
5 Someone I do my job with (2-6)
6 Someone I share an apartment with (8)

2 **Complete the sentences with the correct form of the words in Exercise 1. There is one extra word.**

1 Leah's more of an _____ than a friend. I've only met her a few times.
2 One of my _____ does very little work and expects the rest of us to do it for her.
3 Nicholas likes a tidy home but his _____ is really messy. I don't know how they live together!
4 One of my _____ wants to meet for lunch to discuss work. She pays me a lot of money so I can't say no!
5 I saw my _____ today while I was with my new girlfriend. That was awkward.
6 I'm going out with my sister and _____ tonight. I'm so glad she married him, he's lots of fun.
7 I don't really get on with my _____. She's not at all like my husband. You wouldn't think they had the same parents!
8 My _____ and I are going out to celebrate finishing our course.

Language focus

Introductory *It*

3 **Put the words in the correct order to make sentences.**

1 seems / Lyn and Ellie / me / it / have fallen out / to / that
_____
2 if / going to / it / feels / rain / as / it's
_____
3 that / me / it / a lot of money / we're / strikes / spending
_____
4 though / a hard time / you're / it / as / having / sounds
_____
5 I've / occurs / that / been here before / to me / never / it
_____
6 you've / a great day / looks / if / had / it / as
_____

4 **Choose the correct option a, b or c. More than one option might be possible.**

1 It _____ people spend so much time online these days.
   a bothers me that   **b** alarms me that
   c turns out that
2 It's not that Sam and I don't get on, it's _____ that we don't really know each other.
   a still   **b** yet   **c** just
3 It _____ me that the temperature's getting warmer here each year.
   a strikes   **b** looks   **c** occurs
4 I thought my appointment was today but it _____ it's tomorrow.
   a surprises me that   **b** followed that
   c turns out that
5 It _____ that no one likes my cooking. You aren't eating it!
   a looks as if   **b** appears   **c** feels to me
6 From what you've told me, it _____ you're going to have a great holiday.
   a sounds as though   **b** looks as if
   c feel as though

5 **Complete the second sentence so it means the same as the first.**

1 You don't seem very happy.
   It seems _____ .
2 I realise that the shops close early on a Sunday.
   It occurs _____ .
3 I tried to call you but I didn't have any battery.
   I tried to call you but it turned _____ .
4 I'm surprised that anyone eats this awful fast food.
   It amazes _____ .
5 From what I've seen, this is a lovely house.
   It looks _____ .
6 I'm worried that Tammy always looks fed up.
   It _____ .

Vocabulary
Meetings and discussions

1 Complete the sentences with the words in the box.

> agenda business come gone input item
> move talk through topic

1 Let's see what's on today's meeting _____ .
2 Let's discuss the first _____ on our list.
3 Can we please stay on _____ ?
4 OK, let's get down to _____ .
5 Enough of this small _____ . Let's focus on the big things.
6 I think we've _____ off topic again.
7 We should _____ on to the next topic.
8 I don't think we're going to get _____ everything on the list today.
9 I'd like to have everyone's _____ on this subject.
10 I think we should _____ back to this subject later.

English in action
Lead a discussion and come to a decision

2 Put the words in the correct order to make sentences and questions.

1 down / to / business / get / let's
_____
2 met / Gill / has / from Accounts / everyone ?
_____
3 on / our budget / the agenda / is / item / the next
_____
4 decide on / goal / to / a new project / today / our / is
_____
5 start, / make / we / a / shall / let's ?
_____
6 all / you / Eduardo / know / think / I
_____
7 see / good / here / to / all / you / it's
_____
8 share / purpose of / to / new ideas / is / the / this meeting
_____

3 Correct four words in the meeting introduction.

'It's good to see you all here. Have you all got a copy of the diary for today's meeting? Yes? And has everyone got coffee? Right, let's get begun then. Firstly, I'd like to welcome Jacky from our advertising agency. The role of today's meeting is to think about the next steps of our advertising campaign so it makes sense that Jacky's here. The first object on the agenda is to review how the campaign has been going so far. Jacky, perhaps you could tell us.'

4 Complete the sentences using the prompts in brackets.

1 I'm sorry, I _____ (have / stop). We need to move onto the next topic.
2 Andy, _____ (what / your thoughts) on this subject?
3 I think we _____ (go / off / topic). Let's get back to the item on the agenda.
4 Callie, _____ (maybe / could / tell) us about your project.
5 That's enough about that subject. _____ (let / move) the next agenda item.
6 I'd like _____ (hear / views) on this, Marat.

5 Complete the conversations with phrases a–f.

1 A: So, we've sold 4,000 products so far and …
   B: _____ . I'm not sure that's right.
2 A: Hannah, can you tell us the key points again, please?
   B: Sure. _____ , and we need to get any funding in place by then, too.
3 A: _____ ? I think it's important.
   B: Sure, I'll try and find it now.
4 A: Oh, another thing. What about parking?
   B: _____ . I'm not sure we've got time for it today.
5 A: _____ . Is that right?
   B: Yes, that's it in simple terms.
6 A: I think we need to offer faster online customer support.
   B: Thanks for your input, James. _____ ?

a Do you think you could get hold of that report
b Let me interrupt you there, Mark
c What does everyone else think
d Let's save that for another meeting
e So, just to summarise, we don't have the budget
f Basically, we've got to decide by Friday

Reading

1 **Read the article. Choose the best heading a–d for texts 1–4.**

  a Doctors, but not as we know them

  b Creating superhumans

  c Uploading our feelings

  d The link between health and home

2 **Which writer (1–4) says the following?**

  1 The technology we see in films is unlikely to exist in 30 years' time. _____

  2 Technology is better able to make links between studies than humans. _____

  3 Illnesses we currently face will become insignificant. _____

  4 This technology is in existence now but most people think it's unreasonable. _____

  5 We'll be able to experience things as others do. _____

  6 One person has used this technology to develop a new sense. _____

  7 We'll be able to deal with medical issues before they become a problem. _____

  8 People with disabilities will use this technology to overcome them. _____

  9 The role of a certain profession in society will change. _____

  10 Social media will be forever changed. _____

  11 The technology will help us to consume the right foods. _____

  12 Aspects of a person will never die. _____

3 **Complete the sentences with two or three words in the article.**

  1 According to Adele Carnegie, existing technology could enable the _____ of information between brain cells at some point in the future.

  2 Keigo Shibuya believes that our heart rate will be checked each morning by our _____.

  3 Rohan Anand believes that AI will diagnose us, treat us and send us _____.

  4 Rohan Anand says that artificial intelligence will identify our _____ issues by examining how our bodies react when discussing problems.

  5 Katja Nowak says that one potential problem of biohacking is the fact that people could _____ and control them.

4 **Find phrases 1–8 in the article. Then match them with definitions a–h.**

  1 absorb that emotion _____

  2 monitor our health _____

  3 analyse our saliva _____

  4 potential problem _____

  5 receive treatment _____

  6 cure all major illnesses _____

  7 suffer from _____

  8 overcome physical challenges _____

  a get what you need to stop an illness, e.g. medicine

  b take in that feeling

  c have a disease or medical condition for a long time

  d examine the liquid in our mouths

  e make serious diseases disappear

  f regularly check the condition of our bodies

  g control a problem or disability your body has

  h an issue that might develop in the future

5 **Complete the sentences with the phrases in Exercise 4. Put the verb in the correct form.**

  1 My father _____ back pain.

  2 The doctor _____ to check for allergies and other illnesses yesterday.

  3 We should all _____ by getting a blood test once a year.

  4 I hope that one day doctors can _____ so people don't have to suffer from them anymore.

  5 I'm very sensitive. If I see anyone upset on TV, I immediately _____ and get upset myself.

  6 My sister had to _____ after an accident but she no longer needs a wheelchair.

  7 This mark on my skin is fine but it's a _____ that my doctor's keeping an eye on.

  8 The pharmacist told me I have an eye infection and that I have to see a doctor to _____.

The human body in 2050

It's always fun to look back at a film that predicted life in the year we are in now. Most of the time, the predictions were wrong. After all, none of us are eating pills instead of food, wearing shiny spacesuits that regulate our temperature or getting scanned from top to bottom when we get out of bed. We've asked four futurists to tell us their predictions about 30 years' time to see if they can do better than the film-makers.

1 Adele Carnegie

It's extremely likely that we'll be able to share emotions and memories with other people so that they'll be able to experience them, too. Clearly, the technology isn't available at the moment, but we have developed techniques which might allow the fast transfer of data across neurons in the future. Sharing online will never be the same again. Whenever we share a photo online, we'll be able to embed either the memory or the emotion within it. When someone views the photo, they can absorb that emotion or memory to truly experience it. A person's memories and feelings will live on beyond the person themselves.

2 Keigo Shibuya

We've all seen sci-fi films where the spaceship doctor waves a handheld machine over a person to scan them and find out what's wrong with them. Well, I doubt we'll have this in 30 years but I do think we'll use technology much more to monitor our health. For example, our bathroom mirror will examine the colour of our skin and check our pulse, the floor will weigh us and our toothbrush will analyse our saliva. The technology will find any potential problem and send a warning so we can receive treatment before we get sick. The information will also be used by our kitchens to make recommendations about the kind of food and drink we need to consume so that we're in perfect shape for the day ahead.

3 Rohan Anand

It is probable that artificial intelligence will allow us to cure all major illnesses. How? By being able to read research from around the world and make the connections that humans are unable to. These connections will help us to fully understand the cause of the diseases and how to both prevent and cure them. Serious health issues we suffer from now will become as minor as the common cold. Human doctors will no longer work as they do now. In fact, most of us will communicate with AI when we visit a hospital. It will diagnose us, treat us and send us on our way. This goes for both physical and psychological issues. AI will be able to detect our physical responses when we talk about our problems and better understand where the main psychological problems are.

4 Katja Nowak

Biohacking will be something that more of us do. Already, people are inserting technology into their bodies to make them stronger or to increase their senses. Take the man who has a microchip under his skin which vibrates every time he faces north, for example. The technology allows him to enhance his sense of direction. At the moment, people who do this are considered to be extreme. But in the future, people with physical challenges might use this technology to overcome their difficulties. Of course, this probably won't come without problems of its own. If we hack our bodies, others will be able to hack them, too.

7

Listening

1 🔊 **7.01** **Listen to a radio interview and complete the sentences.**

1 FIRE stands for 'financially independent,
_____ early'.

2 Being financially independent means that you don't need a _____ .

3 Scott and his partner budgeted and saved carefully over _____ years.

4 They had _____ rather than holidays.

5 Now that they're financially independent, they enjoy spending time with their _____ .

2 **Listen again and complete the notes.**

> ### To become financially independent
>
> ✓ Select an appropriately-sized [1]_____ . Nothing too big.
>
> ✗ No [2]_____ , e.g. for a vehicle, getting married, etc.
>
> ✓ Save [3]_____ percent of your income.
>
> ✗ No fancy [4]_____ out, cars or [5]_____ .
>
> ✓ Make your own [6]_____ every day.
>
> ✓ Stay at home for holidays or go [7]_____ . It's cheaper!
>
> ✓ Put savings into a bank account with a high rate of [8]_____ .
>
> ✓ Invest money so that you get a second [9]_____ .
>
> Remember! Some people feel lost when they retire early because they have no [10]_____ or colleagues.

3 **Which of these things do you think a financially independent person might say?**

1 I only just get by with my salary from month to month.

2 I have to live carefully but I feel less stressed.

3 I try to put aside as much as I can each month for the future.

Writing

1 🔊 **7.02** **Listen to a meeting about a local event and correct five mistakes in the notes.**

> ## Street party
>
> ### Date
> • Last w/e in March
>
> ### Location
> • Hill Street – best c/f other roads
> • Put posters thru Hill Street residents' doors re. road closure
>
> ### Guests and tickets
> • Village residents invited, approx. 65 ppl
> • Tickets ↑ £10 pp?
>
> ### Food & drink
> • Guests bring own + Annie to ask three cafés in town to provide some
>
> ### Tables and chairs
> • From village hall + Hill Street residents bring own if nec.
>
> ### Entertainment
> • Mark's brother to DJ
>
> ### Other
> • Lisa to get road closure paperwork from council
> • Meet this time next wk to discuss advertising and DJ

2 Read the notes again. Are the sentences true (T) or false (F)?

1 The notes are organised under headings to make information clear. ....
2 The notes are organised using bullet points to make information clear. ....
3 The notes include full, grammatically-correct sentences including articles and auxiliary verbs. ....
4 The notes include abbreviations. ....
5 The notes include no punctuation. ....
6 The writer uses [name] + to + infinitive to describe an action someone will take. ....

3 Find abbreviations in the notes that mean the same as the words and phrases in the box.

> about/regarding and/plus approximately
> compared with increase necessary people
> price/cost through week weekend

4 Look at the words in the box. How do you think people might abbreviate them? Then read the Focus box and check your ideas.

> because decrease especially information
> number very with without

Using abbreviations in notes

When you take notes, it can save you a lot of time if you use abbreviations for common longer words. This is a list of the most common abbreviations that people use to make notes.

+ = and/plus	thru = through
approx. = approximately	v. = very
b/c = because	wk = week
cf. = compared with	w/e = weekend
esp. = especially	w/ = with
etc. = and so on	w/o = without
i.e. = in other words	x = times (e.g. 2x per week)
info. = information	< = less than
NB = don't forget!	> = greater than
nec. = necessary	→ = leads to/causes
no. = number	✓ = good
ppl = people	↑ = increase
£/€/$ = price/cost	↓ = decrease
re. = regarding	

5 Improve the meeting notes by replacing words with abbreviations where possible and removing articles, pronouns, auxiliary verbs and main verbs *be* and *have*.

> ### Sales
> ① The demand for our products this month is higher than last month.
> ② Our sales this year are low compared with last year.
> ③ Sales have decreased by 30 percent.
> ④ We have no other sales information because Maria is off sick.
>
> ### Advertising
> ⑤ We need to do more to advertise in local newspapers, online and so on.
>
> ### New products
> ⑥ We need a meeting with Tom about our new product.
> ⑦ The promotion of the product is very important.
> ⑧ Don't forget Tom's on holiday next week.

Prepare

6 🔊 7.03 Listen to six people giving information at six different meetings. Write notes for each one.

1 ....
2 ....
3 ....
4 ....
5 ....
6 ....

Write

7 🔊 7.04 Listen to parents Lynne and Ben discussing their upcoming family holiday. Make a list of the things they need to do to get ready for their trip. Use headings, short sentences and abbreviations where possible.

....
....
....
....
....
....
....

Vocabulary

Events in films

1 Choose the correct alternatives.

1 If you *trap/trick* someone, you lie to them to make them do something.

2 If you *rescue/survive* something, you don't die and continue to live.

3 If you *abandon/capture* someone, you catch them and keep them prisoner.

4 If you *rescue/survive* someone, you save them from danger.

5 If you *confront/trap* someone, you face them and challenge them.

6 If you *abandon/overcome* a problem, you deal with it successfully.

2 Complete the film summary with the correct form of the verbs in the box.

| betray | capture | face | go on a mission |
| murder | rescue | survive | trick |

Getting Justice tells the predictable story of private investigator Steve (actor Mike Daniels) whose wife was ¹_____ by a gang of criminals. Determined to get justice, he ²_____ to find his wife's killers and ³_____ them. Along the way, he elicits the help of a pretty waitress (played by Jennifer Williams) and a young teenager (newcomer Tyson Daniels). Unfortunately, the teen ⁴_____ our detective by telling the gang that Steve is close to finding them. What happens next has been seen many times before. Spoiler alert! Someone is ⁵_____ into doing something they shouldn't and they get into a life-threatening situation, but the good guy ⁶_____ them. Someone ⁷_____ a potentially dangerous car explosion and, in the end, the good guy and the bad guy ⁸_____ each other. I doubt you'll be surprised at who wins the day.

Grammar

Second conditional

3 Match the sentence halves.

1 You're sick? If I were you, _____

2 If I had a car, _____

3 We could all go home _____

4 If Dan was more organised, _____

5 If someone had shouted at me like that, _____

6 Would you live abroad _____

7 Were I offered the position, _____

8 Could you see the sea _____

a if the boss left early.

b if that building wasn't in the way?

c things wouldn't be in such a mess.

d I'd go back to bed.

e if you had the chance?

f I might consider taking it.

g I could give you a lift to town.

h I might feel pretty annoyed with them.

4 Choose the correct option a, b or c. More than one option might be possible.

1 Jenny _____ you if you gave her a call.
   a would help   b helped   c will help

2 We _____ to London by train if you didn't want to drive.
   a 'd go   b wouldn't go   c could go

3 I _____ that, if I were you. It's not safe.
   a might do   b would do   c wouldn't do

4 If I _____, I'd love to be able to make my own clothes.
   a would   b could   c might

5 What car would you buy if you _____ the money?
   a would have   b had   c won

6 If I _____ my cat, I think I'd be a bit lonely.
   a had   b didn't have   c wouldn't have

5 Complete the forum comments using the prompts in brackets.

Frank71	So, most important question of the day. If ¹_____ _____? (you / be / in a film / what / be)
Simon	²_____ (I / be) in *Harry Potter*. Just think of all the thin I ³_____ (can / do / if / have) magical powers!
Aria	I'd love to fly a jet plane so maybe *Top Gun* ⁴_____ (if / I / have / the chance).
Lisa	*Frozen* ⁵_____ (be) my first choice, but I can't sing and ⁶_____ (I / make) everyone's ears bleed!
MaxmiLLian	I guess it ⁷_____ (be) fun to play James Bond
Noel	If ⁸_____ (I / have) a willing dance partner, ⁹_____ (I / be) in one of those old musicals from the 1940s
Jen	I ¹⁰_____ (fight) alongside all the Avengers. ¹¹_____ (if / I / can / have) any superpower, ¹²_____ (it / be) X-ray vision.

Vocabulary
Searching and hiding

1 **Put the letters in the correct order. The first letter is in bold.**

1 I just *to**s**pdet* James. He's over there in the corner.
_____

2 Police have *dcar**t**e* the car seen in the video and have arrested the owner. _____

3 Famous people often try to *esgi**d**usi* themselves using hats and sunglasses. _____

4 Police are *sng**p**ruiu* a man driving the wrong way along the motorway. _____

5 If we *ade**h** or**f*** the beach, we might find Ellie there.
_____

6 Detectives are trying to *fiyde**t**ni* a woman seen stealing a car on camera. _____

7 A man has *cie**d**edev* several people by claiming he needs money for medical treatment. _____

8 Detectives are *ci**t**ngrka* a man's mobile phone after he disappeared. _____

2 **Read the text and choose the correct option a, b, or c.**

> **An unexpected return**
>
> When Matt Barker disappeared during a boat trip in 2012, no one expected him to turn up five years later claiming he'd lost his memory. Rescuers had **1**_____ for him alive or dead but had found only his backpack.
>
> Three months before Barker returned, police had received information that suggested he might be alive. They **2**_____ his wife Liz to the south of France where she'd recently moved and **3**_____ her while **4**_____ her husband at the same time. When Barker returned, the story made national headlines. A few people came forward and **5**_____ him as someone they'd met using a different name over the last few years. On top of that, a photo of him and Liz in the south of France the year before was **6**_____ online.
>
> It turned out that Barker had spent much of the five years living secretly in his family home, despite his children believing him to be dead. Both Matt and Liz were found guilty of **7**_____ an insurance company and receiving tens of thousands of pounds illegally. They were sentenced to five years in prison.

1 a examined   b hunted   c traced
2 a traced   b found   c come across
3 a evaluated   b searched for   c kept an eye on
4 a pursuing   b deceiving   c searching
5 a disguised   b identified   c notice
6 a spotted   b witnessed   c tracked
7 a disguising   b trapping   c deceiving

Grammar
Conditionals in the past

3 **Put the words in the correct order to make sentences. The first word(s) are in bold.**

1 university, / a teacher / hadn't / wouldn't / **If I** / be / gone to / I
_____
_____

2 decided not to go / might not / if / **We** / have met / that party / I'd / to
_____
_____

3 right now / I / so much food / **I'd** / if / hadn't eaten / feel OK
_____
_____

4 hello / seen / have come / I would / you, / **If** / I'd / and said
_____
_____

5 filled the car up / **We** / run out of petrol / have / you'd / wouldn't / if
_____
_____
_____

6 hadn't / the traffic / right now / in my car / **I'd still** / if / warned me / you / be sitting / about
_____
_____
_____

7 may have / earlier, / we'd got here / a better seat / **If** / got / we
_____
_____

8 told you Harry / have come / might not / if I'd / would be here / **You**
_____
_____

4 **Complete the sentences with the correct form of the verbs in brackets to make past conditionals.**

1 I _____ (lost) you if you _____ (not hear) me shout.

2 If she _____ (listen) more carefully, she _____ (not/misunderstood).

3 I _____ (feel) more awake right now if I _____ (have) more sleep last night.

4 You _____ (be) so red if you _____ (not/sit) out in the sun all day.

5 We _____ (might not/hit) that traffic jam if we _____ (leave) earlier.

6 It _____ (be) quicker if we _____ (take) the train.

7 If I _____ (study) harder, I _____ (be) better prepared for tomorrow's test.

8 If you _____ (message) me, I _____ (not/have to) call you!

8c

Vocabulary
Visual art

1 Match the words in box A with the words in box B to make words and phrases.

| A | abstract land oil original still water |

| B | artwork artwork colour life painting scape |

2 Choose the correct alternatives.
1 'Do you need a new brush before you start on your *oil painting/print*?'
2 'We need some glue if we're going to make a *collage/landscape*.'
3 'Anyone can throw paint across a canvas and refer to it as abstract *artwork/installation*!'
4 'This is *an original artwork/a statue* by my niece. No fake paintings here!'
5 'I love the colour of the sea in this *portrait/landscape*.'
6 'You can make *sketches/statues* from wood, stone, marble and so on.'
7 'Artists often find it difficult to get the hands right in a *portrait/still life*.'
8 'I really enjoyed walking around the *collage/installation* and hearing the sounds.'

3 What type of art is each person talking about?
1 'I'd say that the *Mona Lisa* is probably the most famous example.' _____
2 'The colours in these paintings tend to be less bright than those in oil paintings.' _____
3 'I love the way that the artist has carved the stone so smoothly.' _____
4 'I don't understand how a load of bricks sitting in the middle of a room is art.' _____
5 'This picture of a cup and saucer looks almost like a photograph.' _____
6 'It's amazing how some artists can draw something perfectly using just a pencil.' _____
7 'We obviously couldn't afford the original for our living room, but this copy is just as good.' _____
8 'I love the way we all look at it and see something completely different.' _____

Language focus
Linkers of concession

4 Choose the correct endings, a or b.
1 The concert started too late for me. Nevertheless,
   a we enjoyed it.   b it was tiring.
2 Although we'd seen it before, the exhibition
   a was still surprising.   b was as expected.
3 We still hoped to go to the concert even though
   a tickets had sold out.   b there were tickets left.
4 I'm not really a fan of installations. However, I
   a didn't like this one much.   b quite liked this one.
5 In spite of never painting before, I thought Richard did
   a a fairly rubbish job.   b a decent job.

5 Make sentences using the prompts. Add the correct punctuation.
1 Despite / fact / the museum / be / in need of repair / it / be / a gorgeous building.
   _____
2 I / want / like / still life / however / I / find / boring.
   _____
3 Although / fake paintings / be / not / original / they / be / still / art.
   _____
4 I / can't / do simple drawings / in spite of it / be / easy for many people.
   _____
5 Watercolours / not / appeal to me / even though / they / be / very popular.
   _____

6 Complete the conversation with phrases a–f.
A: What did you think of the play yesterday?
B: I thought the main actor was a bit wooden, although **1** _____.
A: I really liked him. I loved the dialogue, too, in spite of the fact that **2** _____.
B: Oh yeah, there was that one guy who really mumbled. Even though **3** _____, it's not great if you're sitting at the back!
A: Ha, yeah. Despite **4** _____, I did enjoy it.
B: Me too. I think it's good to go and see a play once in a while despite it **5** _____.
A: I agree. It was worth the price. Nevertheless, **6** _____ to attract a wider audience.

a the lack of clear audio
b they should try to keep the cost of tickets low
c I couldn't always hear it
d it's supposed to be an authentic style of acting
e costing quite a lot of money
f I can see why he's popular

Listening

1 🔊 **8.01** Listen to a discussion between Luke and Sofia. Which one is not a fan of street art?

2 Listen again and choose the correct option, a, b or c.

1 Sofia and Luke agree that the graffiti they see
a is an example of art.
b is unattractive.
c is well positioned.

2 Luke believes that
a all graffiti is art.
b most graffiti is art.
c some graffiti is art.

3 Luke reminds Sofia that
a humans have had a writing system for centuries.
b graffiti has been in existence for a very long time.
c people have always decorated their homes with art.

4 Sofia believes that graffitiing
a is a pointless crime.
b involves necessary risk taking.
c can damage the look of a place.

5 Luke prefers street art which
a brightens up a place.
b is similar to what you'd find in a gallery.
c combines creativity with intelligence.

6 Luke and Sofia both agree that street artists
a need more places to paint.
b help to develop a sense of community.
c ought to think more about building owners.

3 Listen again and complete the sentences.

1 Sofia questions whether a drawing of a
.... on a piece of paper is art.

2 Luke says that he wouldn't be interested in displaying
well-known .... in his home.

3 Luke says that graffiti has existed since
.... began.

4 Luke isn't only interested in street art because it
prevents an area from appearing ....

5 Luke doesn't think a lot of street art would be the same
in a ....

6 Sofia explains that street artists can cause
.... to lose their freedom.

7 Sofia says that she'd heard it's expensive to hire
.... to look after street art.

8 Sofia suggests that for a community to be secure,
everyone needs to ....

4 Match the words in bold with meanings a–h.

1 Anything that someone has the **freedom** to create
is art. ....

2 It's still art because that person **expressed themselves**
through their name. ....

3 (People in caves) at least drew pictures that
represented their lives. ....

4 I'm sure if (people in caves) had written language,
they'd have made political **statements**. ....

5 I think the key issue for me is that graffiti's **against
the law**. ....

6 I'd like to see more **legal** places where artists can
create art. ....

7 You have people coming to **stare at** (the street art). ....

8 Freedom comes with responsibility and an artist needs
to take that **responsibility** seriously. ....

a illegal
b something you say or write that tells people about a
fact or your opinion
c say what you think or feel
d allowed by law
e show something
f a duty to do something or be in charge of something
g the ability to do what you want without being controlled
h look at something for a long time without moving your
eyes

5 Which opinions probably belong to Luke (L) and which
to Sofia (S)?

1 People who graffiti should be fined. ....

2 Street art is diverse. ....

3 Street art allows ordinary people to give their view
on the world. ....

4 Street paintings are at least more interesting than
name graffiti. ....

Reading

1 **Read the article. Put topics a–f in the order they appear in the article.**
- **a** Be careful about what we upload ....
- **b** See what's online about ourselves ....
- **c** Control who can see things we post ....
- **d** Why people want our data ....
- **e** Search for information anonymously ....
- **f** Get rid of unwanted accounts ....

2 **Read the article again. Choose the correct option a, b or c.**

1 In paragraph 1, the writer says that
- **a** we need to care more about privacy than enjoyment online.
- **b** not everyone wants to use our data legally.
- **c** people don't usually mind companies collecting our data.

2 The writer thinks that
- **a** people are sometimes shocked after searching for themselves online.
- **b** we can get a full understanding of what's online by searching our names.
- **c** most of us are fine about what we find online about ourselves.

3 According to the writer,
- **a** companies use us to make money long after we register with them.
- **b** it can be fun to see images of us online pop up years later.
- **c** there's nothing we can do if we're unable to erase an online account.

4 The writer suggests that
- **a** changing our privacy settings isn't worth the time.
- **b** not all social media sites let us change our settings.
- **c** we should use our right to change privacy settings.

5 In paragraph 5, the writer says that
- **a** most of us have updated our social media profiles over the years.
- **b** we should pick less common security questions to answer when logging in.
- **c** people give away private information online without realising it.

6 It is the writer's belief that
- **a** it's amusing when your partner sees things you've been looking at online.
- **b** a certain feature of a search engine can limit your digital trail.
- **c** few search engines collect data while you search online.

3 **Find words or phrases in the article that mean these things.**
- **1** a situation when you are trying to do several different things correctly (paragraph 1)
- **2** keep/continue at the same level as before (paragraph 1)
- **3** related to a particular person or thing (paragraphs 2 and 3)
- **4** worried by (paragraph 2)
- **5** realise or know a situation exists (paragraph 4)
- **6** really/very (paragraph 5)
- **7** do something as much as you want (paragraph 6)
- **8** a message intended to ruin the surprise of something, especially a film (paragraph 6)

4 **Complete the comments with the words and phrases in Exercise 3.**
- **1** I'm often _____ how much personal information my friends share online. I worry that it's too much.
- **2** I'm not _____ search engines that allow you to search anonymously. What are they?
- **3** I'd like to be able to browse to my _____ without having to stop and change privacy settings.
- **4** The amount of data collected by companies is _____ worrying.
- **5** Don't forget to look at places _____ you, as well as names, e.g. places you worked.
- **6** I like the idea of trying to _____ a good level of privacy, but it's easier said than done.
- **7** I bought a birthday present online. The next day an ad for it popped up and my friend saw it. That was definitely a _____!
- **8** Everything we do in life is a _____ between having fun and not taking risks.

5 **Complete the summary with words or phrases in the article.**

In order to maintain privacy online, we should firstly use a **1** _____ to find out how much information about us is available online. Then, we should **2** _____ any old accounts we don't use any more. If we can't do that, we can think about **3** _____ our profile information so no one knows it's ours. We should change privacy settings so that we lower our **4** _____ as much as possible. We should also take care not to post personal information by accident, e.g. answers to **5** _____ . Finally, we should search online using a certain **6** _____ of a search engine that allows us to do it anonymously.

Reducing our digital footprint

Whenever we do anything online, we leave a digital trail. In this article, IT consultant Martin Clarke looks at ways that we can keep our digital trail to a minimum and protect our privacy.

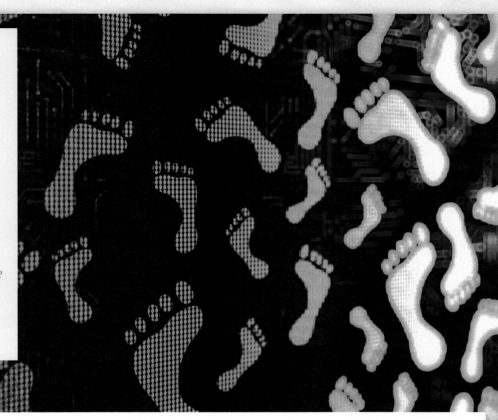

[1]Enjoying the web and keeping a level of privacy is a balancing act. We want to search for and share information with our friends, but without every Tom, Dick and Harry having access to it, too. Businesses want our data to personalise advertising and get us to spend more. A few people want our data for dishonest activities such as identity theft or fraud. So, how exactly can we reduce our digital footprint and maintain our privacy?

[2]The first thing we can do is to search for ourselves using a number of different search engines to find out exactly what others can see about us. However, it's not enough to search just for our names. We need to search for people associated with us to get a true picture. People are often alarmed by what comes up, but it provides motivation for taking action to reduce our online data.

[3]Most of us have registered with websites which we stopped using long ago. By not deleting our accounts with them, they continue to sell data and make a profit from us, or, in the case of social media, old posts still pop up in search engines. To avoid people being able to see embarrassing photos of us at school, we can delete these accounts so that our data is no longer public. If that's not possible, we can consider changing the name and contact details on the account for fake ones so at least they don't associate them with us.

[4]While it might not be easy to delete a social media account, they do have privacy settings that not everyone is aware of. These settings allow us to control exactly who sees what. Other websites have the same controls and, especially if you're living in the EU, you can amend those settings so that they cannot collect data and sell it or share it with their partners. It might be annoying to have to change those settings every time you click on a site, but by taking a few seconds to do so, your digital footprint is reduced or, at least, not increased.

[5]When posting online, we should always think carefully about whether or not we want to share all of the information. We should check our photos carefully. It's surprising how many people give away their address or their car registration number in pictures they post. If we share information such as our pet's name, the school we went to or our favourite food, criminals can guess answers to security questions and access our accounts. Even our social media profiles themselves might give away too much information. It might have seemed OK to tell everyone we were in a relationship when we first registered ten years ago, but do we really want people to know that now? The people truly important to us know that already.

[6]Finally, some search engines offer the opportunity for us to search without our data being collected. This might be called stealth mode or incognito depending on the engine you use. Using this feature is a great way to reduce our digital footprint. We can search to our heart's content without people knowing exactly what we're looking at. After all, it's such a spoiler when you're showing your girlfriend something funny on a website and an advert pops up for the engagement rings you were looking at the other day.

Writing

Spoiler free review:
The end of the game for *The Avengers*

★★★★☆

[1]*Avengers: Endgame* is the final chapter in what has been a decade's worth of stories set in the Marvel universe. The previous film in the series – *Infinity War* – is a hard act to follow with its spectacular storytelling and shocking ending. However, the directors have managed to produce an exciting and satisfying action film that is just as successful.

[2]Directed by Joe and Anthony Russo, the film begins where *Infinity War* ended. The first part of the film is particularly depressing as it centres around our heroes and how they're dealing differently with grief. The plot then focuses on our heroes working together to steal back what they lost in the last film.

[3]While *Infinity War* provided stunning displays of action, *Endgame* takes time to develop the characters. With perhaps too many Marvel films over the last ten years, this cleverly reminds us of why we loved the characters in the first place and why we want them to win over the bad guy. The script is sharp and the plot is quite clever, although there are the usual holes in the plot. Both Ant-Man and Thor, played by Paul Rudd and Chris Hemsworth, add some much-appreciated humour.

[4]At three hours, the film is too long and the action scenes are messier than in previous films. However, they keep you engaged right to the end. While this may not be a perfect film, it is in no way a disappointment and manages to finish the story in a way that both casual viewers and Marvel fans will enjoy.

[5]Get the popcorn, grab a cushion and settle in for the ride. It's worth it.

1 Read the film review. Does the writer think the things in the box are positive (+), negative (−) or both (B)?

the action scenes   focus on characters
the humour   the length of the film
the script   the storyline

2 Match paragraphs 1–5 with purposes a–d. One purpose is used twice.
a Analyse what works well and less well in the film.
b Mention the title and briefly give your opinion.
c Say whether the reader should see the film or not.
d Describe the plot without giving away the ending.

1 _____   2 _____   3 _____   4 _____   5 _____

Including relevant information

A good review of a film or book tries to:

- inform
  It should give basic information, such as the main characters, actors, etc. It should also give basic information about the setting and plot, but it shouldn't try to describe the whole story and it definitely shouldn't contain any spoilers (details that give away the ending).

- judge
  It should explain which elements of the film/book were good and which were not good. It should try to give a reason or evidence for these judgements. The final paragraph should include a decision on whether you recommend the film/book or not.

- entertain
  People enjoy reading reviews if they are well-written and lively. They should include a good range of language and not be too formal.

3 Read the book review. Which two things in the Focus box does it not include?

Elizabeth is missing is a **¹** ____ story which is told from the perspective of a woman in her 80s who's beginning to suffer from dementia, causing her to frequently forget things in the present. **²** ____

Written by Emma Healey, the story centres around Maud's attempts to solve the 70-year-old mystery of her sister Elizabeth's disappearance. Maud remembers that Elizabeth is missing and writes clues in notes to herself that help her to find out why. **³** ____

The story is generally satisfying, switching between past and present very effectively. **⁴** ____ The story also has the ability to bring a tear to your eye when Maud expresses fear and frustration due to her illness.
The ending is clearly explained and makes sense. Having said that, you could argue it is a little predictable. **⁵** ____

4 Complete the book review in Exercise 3 with phrases a–e.

a All in all, the story entertains and is worth the time for those who love to laugh, cry and solve a puzzle.

b The real joy is the humour which Healey puts into Maud's words.

c cleverly written

d The story switches between the present time and 70 years ago.

e It's both sweet and sad and will no doubt appeal to readers who love a good mystery.

5 Complete the sentences with the words in the box.

by	character	explores	illustrates	little-known
played	plot	stars		

1 The part is ____ by actress Gemma McKinnon.
2 This is a novel by a ____ writer called Ben Cardwell.
3 It is directed ____ Steven Spielberg.
4 This ____ the main problem of the story.
5 It ____ a number of well-known actors.
6 The ____ centres around a family.
7 The main ____ is a female head teacher in a struggling school.
8 It ____ the themes of grief and loss.

6 Decide if the sentences in Exercise 5 are about a book, a film or both.

Prepare

7 You're going to write a review of a book or film. Complete these notes.

Name: ____
Author/Director: ____
Set in (time): ____
Set in (place): ____
Main character: ____
Basic plot (without ending):
____
____
____
Positive points:
____
____
____
Negative points:
____
____
____
Your summary:
____
____
____

8 Organise the information into four paragraphs. Choose phrases on this page to use in your review.

Write

9 Write your review.

9A

Vocabulary
Mystery

1 **Look at the headlines and choose the correct alternatives.**

1 Experts say Loch Ness Monster photograph was a *hoax/trick*.

2 **Man killed by wife.** *Motive/Purpose* **unknown.**

3 Police say time wasters *account for/ bring about* 75 percent of emergency calls.

4 Man accused of theft *ends up/turns out* to be victim.

5 30-year old crime *remains/stays* a mystery according to investigators.

6 Police find new *evidence/signs* in the disappearance of Rebecca Hudley.

7 Firefighters investigating hotel fire hunt for *clues/data*.

8 Police *identify/observe* missing man as Henry Williamson.

2 **Match the words and phrases in the box with sentences 1–6.**

clue   evidence   hoax   motive   red herring   victim

1 Detectives spent ages trying to find out who sent the note but, in the end, it was completely irrelevant.
....

2 The thief's fingerprints were found on items in the wallet. ....

3 The photograph is obviously a fake. There's no way that's an alien! ....

4 Sara's been too scared to go out alone since she was attacked. ....

5 If you want to know where Josh is, look online. He always posts photos there. ....

6 We have no idea why anyone would want to steal a really old garden chair. ....

Grammar
Past modals of deduction

3 **Match the sentences that mean the same.**

1 The police found some money in the garden. ....
2 The couple were sleeping upstairs. ....
3 Were there definitely only two thieves? ....
4 The thieves left lots of fingerprints. ....
5 We don't know how they got in. ....

a They can't have been professionals.
b No, there might have been three of them.
c The thieves must have dropped it.
d They could have climbed in through the window.
e They can't have heard anything.

4 **Correct the mistakes in five of the sentences.**

1 It's cold in here. James must had turned the heating off.

2 The train mustn't have gone already. It's only 6.05.

3 I saw Lee in the barber's. He must have been get a haircut.

4 Camila just screamed. She must have been seeing something scary.

5 My phone battery might have run out but I'm not sure.

6 Rob walked right past us. He must have been noticing us.

5 **Read the puzzle and complete the comments with modal verbs and the correct form of the verbs in brackets.**

> There were two fathers and two sons. They walked into a shop and each bought a bar of chocolate for €1. The total for all of the chocolate bars was €3. How was that possible?

Jimmy Well, there ¹............... (be) only three people and not four. It wasn't possible otherwise.

Lia Do you think the father ²............... (be) one person? A father to each son?

Marley They ³............... (buy) a bar of chocolate each. It just doesn't add up.

Grant I'm not sure, but one of the four people ⁴............... (have) two roles.

Lia Ah, right. I'm not sure but one of the fathers ⁵............... (also/be) one of the sons.

Benji The three people ⁶............... (consist) of a grandfather, father and son. That's the only way it works.

Vocabulary

Knowledge

1 Choose the correct options a, b or c.

> **Strange theories: the moon landings are fake**
>
>
>
> Some people ¹_____ that man has never actually landed on the moon. They ²_____ that the moon landings were actually filmed in the desert somewhere on Earth and the film is a ³_____. Their ⁴_____, they say, lies in the film. They've ⁵_____ unusual shadows, the lack of stars in the sky and a flag moving as if there's wind, among other things. These observations have led them to ⁶_____ that NASA cheated in order to win the space race with the USSR. However, none of their scientific ⁷_____ are correct. There are clear explanations for every issue they raise. On top of that, no one's ever been able to actually ⁸_____ that the moon landings weren't real and a lot of people would have needed to lie to keep it a secret.

1	a	consider	b	plan	c	theorise
2	a	misunderstand	b	suspect	c	recognise
3	a	fake	b	copy	c	suspicion
4	a	suggestion	b	assumption	c	proof
5	a	observed	b	glimpsed	c	witnesses
6	a	exclaim	b	conclude	c	assess
7	a	considerations	b	knowledge	c	concepts
8	a	support	b	prove	c	assess

2 Complete the sentences with the correct form of the words in the box.

> assume   conclude   fake   know   misunderstand
> observe   suspect   theory

1 I've got no idea when he'll get here but I _____ it'll be late afternoon.

2 That wasn't what I meant. You must have _____ me.

3 I have to admit that my _____ of history is pretty poor.

4 I don't always feel like smiling at work so I have to _____ it.

5 We came to the _____ that it was time to end our relationship.

6 There are some really interesting _____ about space and time.

7 People make the _____ that I'm confident because I'm friendly, but it's not true.

8 We made several interesting _____ during the experiment.

Grammar

Verb patterns

3 Choose the correct alternatives.

1 I don't mind people *to wear/wearing* their shoes in my house.

2 Jack's persuaded me *giving/to give* up social media for a month.

3 We've arranged *seeing/to see* Mary while we're here.

4 You never let me *do/to do* the washing up.

5 I can't stand *to play/playing* tennis in the rain.

6 We didn't expect you *come/to come* and help us.

7 He finally agreed *riding/to ride* the rollercoaster with us.

8 Can you help me *move/moving* this table?

4 Complete the conversations with the correct form of the verbs in the box.

> be   come   do   fix   go   leave   not/pay   pay
> pick   speak   try   turn

1 **A:** Mrs Jones wants us ¹_____ our music down.
  B: I told you that it ²_____ too loud!

2 **A:** I've agreed ³_____ some gardening for my uncle.
  B: Do you want me ⁴_____ and help you?

3 **A:** I can't stand you ⁵_____ wet towels on the floor!
  B: I'm sorry. I promise that I ⁶_____ them up in future.

4 **A:** The electricity company is saying that we ⁷_____ last month's bill.
  B: Really? I thought I'd asked you ⁸_____ it but maybe not.

5 **A:** I'm trying to persuade you ⁹_____ fishing with me.
  B: I know. I don't mind you ¹⁰_____ but it won't work! I'm not interested.

6 **A:** I want to learn how ¹¹_____ a flat tyre.
  B: I suggest that you ¹²_____ to Bob. He can teach you.

5 Make sentences using the prompts.

1 I / can't / imagine / anyone / enjoy / this music.

2 Susie / want / make / dinner for us.

3 I / just / realise / we've met before.

4 My boss / has / recommend / I apply for a promotion.

5 My parents / make / go to bed really early when I was young.

6 Dan / just / ask / go / to a wedding with him but I can't go.

7 I / assure / this is our lowest possible price.

8 Sophie / just / agree / let / me / cut her hair.

Vocabulary
Common phrasal verbs

1 **Match the sentence halves.**

1 This might not work, so I've already come ....
2 I'm late again. I'll need to come ....
3 Where did you come ....
4 I wasn't looking forward to it but it turned ....
5 I hated letting ....
6 Shall we figure ....
7 I'm sorry but I really need to get ....
8 Haven't you got ....

a across these old photos?
b on with my work.
c out what to do next?
d up with a plan B.
e my friends down at the last minute.
f over that cold yet?
g out a lot better than expected.
h up with another excuse.

2 **Correct the mistakes in the sentences.**

1 Don't make in that it was my fault.
  It was yours!
2 That red tree over really stands up from the others.
3 Lia comes up as a really lovely person.
4 I hate my job but I need to stick it up for the money.
5 It wasn't easy to get everyone in one place but it's turned up OK.
6 It's going to take Giulia a while to get under failing her exams.
7 By failing her exams, she feels that she's let her family up.
8 It's a small problem but we'll figure on the way forward.

Language focus
Phrasal verbs

3 **Match the phrasal verbs in each pair with meanings A–B.**

1 If we let the blind down, there won't be any light in here.
2 I don't want to let my family down.
  A not do something someone expects you to
  B move something to a lower position
3 I think I've finally figured out the answer to this puzzle.
4 I can't figure Jane out. She's a bit unusual!
  A think about a problem until you have the answer
  B understand why someone behaves as they do
5 The world is made up of all kinds of interesting people.
6 My sister once made up a story about being a famous actress.
  A combine together to form something
  B pretend something is true to deceive someone
7 I just can't seem to get over this cold.
8 I tried to get the idea over to my boss.
  A succeed in communicating something to someone
  B become well again after an illness

4 **Put the words in the correct order to make sentences and questions.**

1 silly plan / with / that / came / who / up ?
  ....
2 over / still / the flu / getting / Mike's
  ....
3 my life / need to / get / stop worrying / I / with / and / on
  ....
4 about / make / different stories / how they met / my parents / up
  ....
5 out / certainly / the rest / your orange car / from / stands
  ....
6 the possible / through / carefully / think / consequences / let's
  ....

5 **Complete the article with the correct form of the words in brackets. Add a particle.**

> It's funny how life works out. For years, I'd assumed that I'd get good grades at school, go to university and become a psychologist. So, when I saw my final exam results, it was a shock. I wouldn't be able to study my chosen course. I felt as if I'd [1] .... (let/my family).
> I was embarrassed to tell my friends so I [2] .... (make) that I was taking a year off to help my parents with their business. When my friends had a leaving party before university, I
> [3] .... (make/an excuse) and didn't go.
> After a few weeks of feeling sorry for myself, I realised that I had to
> [4] .... (get/my disappointment) and
> [5] .... (get/with my life). I applied to appear on a reality TV show. I must have [6] .... (stood) from the crowd as I was one of 20 picked from over 3,000 people. I didn't get famous from it, but I did get a job behind the scenes with the TV production company. I love it and so it's all
> [7] .... (turn/well).

Vocabulary

Describing problems with products and services

1 Choose the correct alternatives.

1 My delivery arrived, except the company delivered the *false/wrong* item.

2 The T-shirt I want is out of *shelf/stock* but I'll check again tomorrow.

3 I can't get online. I think the internet's *down/up*.

4 The website said my delivery would come yesterday but it didn't *arrive/reach*.

5 Our gas bill is much higher than *assumed/expected*.

6 Some concert tickets I ordered got *away/lost* in the post.

7 I tried to book a table but the restaurant's *booked/reserved* up all evening.

8 Jeremy tried to pay but his card was *refused/turned down*.

English in action

Explain a problem and ask for action

2 Put sentences a–i in the correct order to make a conversation. The caller speaks first.

a I'm sorry but apparently she's out for lunch at the moment. ....

b I'll just check if she's available. Who shall I say is calling? ....

c Yes, please. Thank you very much. ....

d No problem. ....

e Hello, I was trying to get through to Ava Johnson. ....

f Shall I get her to call you when she gets back? ....

g It's William James. I'm calling about a bill she recently sent me. ....

h Oh, that's a shame. I wanted to ask about payment. ....

i I'll just put you on hold. ....

3 Put the words in order to make sentences and questions.

1 put / to reception, / you / through / please / can / me ?

....

2 concerning / it / what / is ?

....

3 a job application / calling / I'm / about

....

4 through / to Marcus / put / you / I'll

....

5 answer / Stefania / your questions / be able to / will

....

6 someone / help me / there / is / could / who / there ?

....

7 back / you / in a few minutes / call / could ?

....

4 Complete the conversations with the phrases in the box.

> calling about   'd like you   get a call back   got a problem   let me check
> refund the money   the problem is   try and come   would it be possible

1 **A:** I have a brand new washing machine. ¹... that it's not working.

B: OK. Do you need me to come and look at it?

A: Yes, please. ²... to come tomorrow?

B: I can't but I'll ³... on Thursday.

A: OK, great.

2 **A:** I've ⁴... with a book I ordered. It never arrived.

B: Oh dear. ⁵... to see what happened. Ah, right, we're actually out of stock.

A: OK. Could you ⁶... that was taken from my account then?

B: Of course. I'll sort that out for you right away.

3 **A:** I'm ⁷... my new laptop. The battery keeps dying.

B: Oh, I'm sorry to hear that.

A: I ⁸... to take a look at it, please.

B: Yes, of course. I'll refer your request to our engineering department and I'll make sure that you ⁹... in the next 24 hours.

5 Complete the conversations using the prompts in brackets.

1 **A:** Hi, is that the garage?

B: Yes, it is.

A: ¹... (about/my car). It's not starting. ²... (like you/take a look/it).

B: I'm afraid that we're fully booked today but ³... (I/have/word/manager) and see if there's anything we can do.

2 **A:** I've received our electricity bill this morning but ⁴... (must/mistake). It says we owe €234 when we usually pay around €100.

B: ⁵... (let/check/see/what/happened). Right, yes, I think there's an error.

A: ⁶... (want/know/why/that/be).

B: It looks like you've been charged the higher rate.

Reading

1 Read the article. Match headings a–e with paragraphs 1–5.

a Real or fiction? ....

b Survival instinct ....

c A lost flight ....

d A ghost town ....

e A natural desire for answers ....

2 Read paragraphs 1–3 again. Are the sentences true (T) or false (F)?

Roanoke Island

1 Some of the first settlers on Roanoke Island returned home. ....

2 The first settlers got on well with their neighbours. ....

3 The first settlers left the island without leaving a single clue. ....

4 People have imagined various reasons for their disappearance. ....

Agatha Christie

5 Agatha Christie's disappearance got little media attention. ....

6 She left her car and went to a hotel. ....

7 She stayed in the hotel for the whole of the 11 days she was missing. ....

8 She gave little information about her disappearance. ....

Amelia Earhart

9 Amelia Earhart was unable to break any world record. ....

10 She had completed a large part of her journey before she disappeared. ....

11 No one has searched for Earhart's plane. ....

12 One idea is that Earhart wanted to start a new life. ....

3 Read paragraphs 4–5 and choose the correct options a, b or c.

1 The writer says that tales of people's disappearance last for a long time because ....

   a discussing things online has been possible for several years.

   b discovering new things and places are a result of questioning.

   c wanting to know things is a typical human characteristic.

2 According to the writer, people search for information in order to ....

   a continue to live in the world around us.

   b solve interesting problems.

   c avoid feeling annoyed.

3 The writer says that real life is ....

   a more organised than fiction.

   b less organised than fiction.

   c similar to fiction.

4 Find words or phrases in the article that mean these things.

1 the negative way people behave towards each other (paragraph 1)

2 began a search for someone. (paragraph 2)

3 attention that someone gets from media (paragraph 2)

4 stated that something was true (paragraph 2)

5 far from places where other people live (paragraph 3)

6 find out something we want to know (paragraph 4)

7 made it possible for people (paragraph 4)

8 a perfect situation (paragraph 5)

5 Complete the forum comments with the correct form of words and phrases in Exercise 4.

Di
I doubt Christie's disappearance was for ¹............................ . Her books were already popular.

Ava
Did people really ²............................ that the Mary Celeste crew were killed by a giant sea animal? Unbelievable!

Liam
I don't suppose the police would ³............................ with 1,000 officers if I went missing!

Emma
If we didn't want to ⁴............................ our curiosity about the world, we wouldn't have discovered many of the things we have.

Gabriel
The internet has ⁵............................ ordinary people to do research about these disappearances and share ideas.

Luisa
Roanoke Island wasn't a ⁶............................ place so I think the settlers just left and went to find food elsewhere.

The real-life mysteries we want to solve

Unless it's one sock missing from a pair or our phone, mystery disappearances seem to fascinate us. Here, Alexia Smith investigates some of the most well-known and examines why we're so interested in them.

1

There are certain disappearances which have become folklore in western culture. Stories which both fascinate us and frustrate us as we struggle to work out exactly what happened. One of the oldest stories is that of Roanoke Island. In 1858, an English settlement was created in what is now North Carolina in the US. After a year, many of the settlers returned to England due to a lack of food and poor relations with the local tribespeople, leaving behind only a small number of people. By the time a second group of settlers arrived a year later, everyone had disappeared from the settlement, leaving only the word CROATOAN carved into a tree, the name of a local tribe. Theories include murder, disease and starvation.

2

When Agatha Christie went missing in the UK in 1926, it was like a plot from one of her books. Police launched a national manhunt that involved around a thousand police officers searching for her, while her fans held their breath. It even made the news around the world after Christie's car was found abandoned. The media made all kinds of claims – that she'd drowned, been murdered or had only disappeared to get publicity for her new book. In the end, Christie was found at a hotel in the north of the country eleven days later. Locals had spotted her enjoying local dances but hadn't recognised her. Christie claimed that she'd been suffering from memory loss and gave no further clues as to what happened to her. The police were unable to provide an explanation.

3

Amelia Earhart was the first female pilot to fly solo across the Atlantic Ocean. In 1937, she and navigator Fred Noonan left California on what they thought would be the first round-the-world flight. They completed two-thirds of their journey before disappearing somewhere over the Pacific Ocean. Their plane has never been found. One theory is that they crashed and sank, however modern technology has failed to detect the plane despite many attempts. Another theory is that they went off course and landed on a remote island where they survived for some time due to objects found there decades later. A rather more creative theory is that they returned to the US with new identities and became spies.

4

Mysteries like these exist around the world but what makes the stories endure? Even today, you can find forums online with people speculating as to what happened in events decades ago. Theories about our fascination with these events focus on human traits. *Homo sapiens* have been searching for answers for tens of thousands of years in order to satisfy our curiosity. Such curiosity enabled us to make new discoveries, create modern inventions and reach all four corners of the world.

5

Where does this curiosity come from? It's likely to be the result of a biological need to survive. The more we know about our environment, the more chance we have of surviving as a species. To understand our environment, we need to gather all the pieces and put them together, like a jigsaw puzzle. When a piece is missing, it frustrates us because it means we're unable to learn from it. In an ideal world, all of these puzzles would be solved but unfortunately, life just isn't that neat and tidy. Nor is it the ending to an Agatha Christie book.

Listening

1 ◀)) 9.01 **Listen to Abi presenting part of a podcast. What is the purpose of the podcast?**

a To inform the listener on how to do something

b To entertain the listener and make them laugh

c To argue a point of view and provide reasons

2 **Listen again. Choose the correct option, a, b or c.**

1 Abi says that when you appear on a reality TV show, you should _____

a agree to feature in newspapers.

b come across as someone who likes attention.

c do whatever you need to do to get noticed.

2 Abi suggests that YouTube videos go viral when they're _____

a posted at the right time.

b shared with people you know.

c based on something humorous.

3 Abi believes that social media influencers do well when they _____

a engage with the people who follow them.

b choose a general topic.

c avoid posting too often.

4 Abi says that arguing with a famous person online only works if _____

a the person has fans who love them.

b you take care with how you word your criticism.

c your message includes insults.

5 Abi believes that using a skill to become famous _____

a is not particularly worthwhile.

b is more time-consuming than other actions.

c will make you more money.

Writing

1 **Read the essay on page 75. What is the writer's point of view? How do you know?**

a Celebrities make poor role models

b Celebrities used to make good role models

c Celebrities make good role models today

2 **Match purposes a–c with paragraphs 1–5. Then read the Focus box and check your answers.**

a Present a reason to support an opinion.

b Summarise your opinion again and give a final thought.

c Introduce the topic and present an opinion.

1 _____   2 _____   3 _____   4 _____   5 _____

Structuring a simple discursive essay

Introduction

Mention both sides of the argument. Give your own opinion. Try to make it a strong opinion.

It is easy to see why many people believe that
Despite this, I believe …

Main paragraphs

Include at least three main points, each with its own paragraph. Each paragraph should begin with a topic sentence that summarises the point of the paragraph. Follow up the topic sentence with examples or supporting ideas.

First and foremost, …
Furthermore, it is a fact that …
There is no doubt that …

Conclusion

State your opinion again in a different way. Finish with a final thought.

In summary, …
In conclusion, …
To summarise, …

3 **Match the alternative topic sentences a–c with paragraphs 2–4.**

a Celebrities use their position to raise awareness of certain issues.

b Celebrities still have an essential place in our lives today.

c Regardless of the type of work they do, the work of a celebrity is challenging.

2 _____   3 _____   4 _____

Are today's celebrities good role models?

[1]It is easy to see why many people criticise today's celebrities. In the past, they were almost always celebrated for some kind of achievement but these days, many are celebrated just for the way they look. Despite this, I believe the majority of celebrities make good role models.

[2]First and foremost, there is no doubt that the majority of celebrities work hard despite the nature of their work. It might not seem difficult to model or to promote a new perfume, but it actually takes a lot of effort to create a personal brand and make money from it. When other people see this effort, they learn that nothing is easy and everything requires hard work.

[3]Furthermore, celebrities often use their fame to speak out on particular topics. By doing this, they highlight causes which are important in society such as equal rights or mental health issues. They also encourage others to give to people in need by donating large amounts of money to charity themselves. This promotes and encourages the helping of others.

[4]Finally, celebrities continue to fulfil an important role in society today. Not everyone has a person around them that is able to inspire them in the right way. If your dream is to become a sports star or a musician, you usually need to look outside of your family. If you suffer from anxiety when no one in your family does, a celebrity who suffers from the same thing can help you to feel as if you are not alone and you can succeed. Any celebrity that inspires another person to act positively is a role model.

[5]In conclusion, while not all celebrities can be defined as good role models, the majority of them work hard at what they do. That may be winning gold medals at an Olympic Games or it may be making humorous videos online. Whichever it is, these celebrities are able to model positive behaviour which others can admire and then copy. This makes them an important part of our society. After all, we all need role models to inspire us in life.

4 Put the words in the correct order to make useful phrases for an essay.

1 evidence / that / plenty of / is / there ...

2 addition / that / in / to ...

3 summary, / in ...

4 convinced / am / that / I ...

5 summarise, / to

6 proof / that / this / conclusive / is ...

7 believe / that / strongly / I ...

8 main / that / is / reason / the ...

5 Are the useful phrases in Exercise 4 best used in the introduction (I), main paragraphs (M) or conclusion (C) of an essay?

I .... M .... C ....

Prepare

6 Read the statement below. Are you for or against it? Why? Make notes.

Professional sports stars are paid too much money.

7 Plan a discursive essay about the statement in Exercise 6. Use this structure to help you.

Introduction
Paragraph 2:
Main point
Supporting evidence/example
Additional supporting idea
Paragraph 3:
Main point
Supporting evidence/example
Additional supporting idea
Paragraph 4:
Main point
Supporting evidence/example
Additional supporting idea
Conclusion

Write

8 Write your discursive essay.

10A

Vocabulary

Personal fulfilment

1 **Complete comments a–c with the phrases in the box.**

> artistic ability   my great passion   like-minded friends
> place I can call home   a place of my own
> sense of adventure   my soul mate   my true vocation
> unique talent

a 'I've had a few different jobs, but none of them have been **1**_____ . I'm still looking for that. **2**_____ is gaming. I love it but it's not easy to turn it into a paid job. The online gaming community's great though and I've made a few **3**_____ there.'

b 'I wish I had some kind of **4**_____ _____ but I can barely draw a stick man, let alone paint amazing pictures. My **5**_____ _____ is being able to touch my nose with my tongue, hardly anything to shout about!'

c 'I've always had a **6**_____ so I spend much of my time travelling around different countries. I don't have **7**_____ anywhere in the world. I stay with friends. One day, if I meet **8**_____ , I might settle down in one place and finally get a **9**_____ .'

2 **Complete the sentences with one word. The first letter is given to help you.**

1 There are a set of **c**_____ principles that most of us live by.

2 I'm still not sure what my purpose in **l**_____ is.

3 Teaching is my true **v**_____ in life.

4 I never felt a **s**_____ of belonging until I met my university friends.

5 I think that Mel and Bex belong together. They're true **s**_____ mates.

6 I'm getting my own flat next week. A place I can call **h**_____ .

7 Dan's never had much of a sense of **a**_____ . He never goes anywhere.

8 Georgina can persuade anyone to do anything. It's a **u**_____ talent.

Grammar

Future perfect and future continuous

3 **Match the sentence halves.**

1 What will you be _____

2 Do you think Andy will have _____

3 When I next see you, I'll be _____

4 I hope you'll _____

5 Anna will more than likely have _____

6 I would think I'll be _____

7 Archie almost certainly won't have _____

8 Will you be _____

a seeing Murat later?

b doing in ten years' time?

c wearing my wedding dress!

d asked you to marry him by the end of the year?

e tidied his room by the time we get home.

f have had a haircut by the time I see you next!

g got her degree by the time you see her.

h doing the same things this time next year.

4 **Correct five mistakes in the sentences.**

1 Will you be see Dana later?

2 I suspect that we'll be still waiting for the bus in half an hour.

3 I have finished this report by the end of the day.

4 Where will Samuel be going on his travels?

5 I'll more than likely have leave before you get here.

6 I doubt Stefan will have lived in his flat this time next year.

5 **Complete the conversations with the correct future form of the verbs in brackets.**

1 **A:** Do you think we **1**_____ (still/work) here in five years' time?

   B: No, I think we **2**_____ (get) jobs elsewhere by then.

2 **A:** **3**_____ (you/go) to the supermarket later?

   B: Not specifically but I **4**_____ (pass) one if you need me to get something.

3 **A:** When do you think you **5**_____ (finish) this book?

   B: I doubt I **6**_____ (read) it all before next week. It's long!

4 **A:** **7**_____ (you/still/work) in an hour?

   B: No, I **8**_____ (probably/finish) before then.

5 **A:** I hope we **9**_____ (not/live) here for long. There's no space.

   B: Don't worry. I think we **10**_____ (move) somewhere bigger by the end of the year.

10B

Vocabulary

Fame

1 Choose the correct alternatives.

1 The band have finally had their *big break/ legacy*.
2 She's relatively *high profile/ unknown* but I think she'll be big soon.
3 That new actor everyone's talking about has *gone unnoticed/ taken the world by storm*.
4 None of us predicted that the show would be *an instant hit/ in the public eye* with viewers.
5 My dad *shot to fame/ started out* as a musician in the 80s but was never well-known.
6 I guess that most people want to leave behind a *legacy/ big break* that will live on.
7 Not everyone enjoys *being in the public eye/ taking the world by storm* when they get famous.

2 Match the sentence halves.

1 The song was an instant _____
2 Tom got his big _____
3 Maxine shot to _____
4 The band have left a long-lasting _____
5 Being in the public _____
6 Ed Sheeran is a high _____

a fame after appearing on radio.
b hit with listeners.
c legacy in the music industry.
d break on a reality show.
e profile singer.
f eye isn't always easy.

3 Choose the correct option a, b or c.

> **The music hall of fame: not a quick path**
>
> It sometimes feels as if musicians **1**_____ to fame overnight. One day, they're completely **2**_____ . The next day, they're all over the internet. The truth is that few bands and singers are lucky enough to have **3**_____ hit. Most of them go **4**_____ for years before they finally get their big **5**_____ . Some of the most high-**6**_____ bands spent years playing to tiny audiences before they eventually took the world by **7**_____ and play to thousands. Occasionally, a band will be discovered shortly after **8**_____ out, but often they disappear just as quickly as they appeared, never to be heard of again.

	a		b		c
1	a lead	b	travel	c	shoot
2	a unknown	b	secret	c	anonymous
3	a a sudden	b	an instant	c	a quick
4	a unnoticed	b	unseen	c	unrecognised
5	a opportunity	b	access	c	break
6	a profile	b	famous	c	known
7	a force	b	storm	c	success
8	a beginning	b	becoming	c	starting

Grammar

Articles

4 Correct the mistakes in the sentences.

1 Cats are much easier pets than dog.
2 Can you pass me one of a plates, please?
3 Our car broke down near the Chicago.
4 Could you tell me where a police station is, please?
5 That's a most amazing thing I've ever heard!
6 The inner beauty is more important than outer beauty.
7 I'd love to go on a safari across Sahara Desert.
8 Who's that man? One with the black cap.

5 Complete the facts using the prompts in brackets.

> **Facts to wow your friends with**
>
> - Did you know that carrots are naturally yellow, white or purple? **1**_____ (Dutch/breed/orange carrots) in the 17th century as a tribute to their King, William of Orange.
> - In 2012, **2**_____ (British town of Dull/link with/American town of Boring) in Oregon. Together, they are Dull and Boring.
> - Apollo 11, **3**_____ , (spaceship/which land/moon) had less computing power than a washing machine.
> - In their lifetime, **4**_____ (person/get rid of/about 35 kg/skin).
> - In 2009, physicist Stephen Hawking **5**_____ (threw/party for/time travellers) but he **6**_____ (not/ send/invitations) until 2013 to see if time travel existed. No one **7**_____ (turn up to/party).
> - In **8**_____ (Middle Ages/ in/Europe), **9**_____ (moment/was/equal to/90 seconds). That's because **10**_____ (hour/be/ divided into/40 moments).

Language focus
Compound adjectives

1 Match the words in box A with the words in box B to make compound adjectives.

A	densely- good- five- hard- high- middle- part- self- strong- well-

B	aged confident educated looking populated tech time up willed year

2 Choose the correct alternatives.

1 This medication can have some *long/short*-term effects but they don't last.
2 My mum's quite well-*know/known* in our town.
3 I'm just going to take a five-*minute/moment* break.
4 This area's quite *build/built*-up, isn't it?
5 My children are usually well-*behaved/educated* in public.
6 Bobby's so *absent/narrow*-minded. He's not open to new ideas at all.
7 My aunt lives in quite a *broken/run*-down house.
8 Anya is quite self-*confident/centred*. She only ever thinks of herself.

3 Complete the conversations with the compound adjectives in the box.

15-year absent-minded brightly-lit broken-down internet-connected part-time so-called state-of-the-art well-known well-off

1 A: This isn't a very **1** _____ room.
  B: There's a lamp over here. That might help.
2 A: Shall we get rid of this?
  B: Yeah. Who needs a **2** _____, old vacuum cleaner?
3 A: Let's ask Tom to come on holiday with us.
  B: I'm not sure he can afford it. He's not that
  3 _____ at the moment.
4 A: I can't find my keys again.
  B: Grr, you're so **4** _____. Pay more attention!
5 A: Wow, your TV is huge!
  B: Yes, it's a **5** _____ 175 cm
  6 _____ TV.
6 A: It's a **7** _____ fact that women are safer drivers than men.
  B: Safer, perhaps – but better, no!
7 A: How old do you have to be to get a
  8 _____ job while at school?
  B: I think it's 16 although I know a
  9 _____ -old who has one.
8 A: What do you think about Sally's
  10 _____ hobby?
  B: Well, it might not be much of a hobby to you but it makes her happy.

Vocabulary
Persuasion and enforcement

4 Put the letters in brackets in the correct order to complete the sentences.

1 It's hard to _____ (coneref) laws without police on the streets.
2 If we _____ (laslint) security cameras outside the factory, it should stop trespassers.
3 Anyone who climbs over the fence should be _____ (dfein) at least £200.
4 The government should _____ (ricedunto) a new law to stop us using phones in the street.
5 The town council have _____ (utp pu) some signs about the new road laws.
6 We should _____ (craghe) extreme sports people for any emergency services they need.
7 Our teachers _____ (datecued) us about online dangers.
8 Parents should _____ (carousedig) their children from taking silly risks.

5 Choose the correct option a, b or c.

Jon   I'm really fed up with walkers going up the mountain without the proper clothing, water or food, and then having to be rescued from the mountain.
Anna I know what you mean. They should be **1** _____ quite a lot of money for walking in bad weather, too.
Jon   The local government should **2** _____ some kind of law about walkers needing a guide with them.
Anna That's quite extreme. A lot of walkers are experienced. And how will the government **3** _____ it? There are no police at the bottom of the mountain ready and waiting for walkers who don't understand the dangers.
Jon   They could **4** _____ cameras there or something.
Anna Sure, but even then, they can't stop people, just record who they are. The only way to change people's behaviour is by **5** _____ them about the dangers.
Jon   How can we do that? It's not enough to **6** _____ a few notices that try to **7** _____ people from going unprepared. No one ever reads them.
Anna OK, then, maybe we could **8** _____ people money for entering the mountain area from the car park. After all, it's a national park. That way, when they need rescuing, there's money to cover the cost.
Jon   That's not a bad idea, actually.

1	a disciplined	b punished	c fined
2	a introduce	b start	c develop
3	a instruct	b order	c enforce
4	a put on	b install	c set
5	a educating	b coaching	c training
6	a raise	b put up	c attach
7	a encourage	b discourage	c persuade
8	a request	b claim	c charge

Listening

1 🔊 **10.01 Listen to a science podcast. Are these common scientific beliefs a fact or fiction?**

1 We currently only use 10 percent of our brains.
2 Lightning doesn't strike the same thing twice.
3 If you drop a penny from the Empire State Building, it can seriously hurt someone.
4 Water goes down the drain in the opposite direction if you're in the southern hemisphere.
5 A goldfish only has a three-second memory.

2 Listen again and answer the questions.

1 How much of our brain do we use?

2 If we say 'lightning doesn't strike twice', what do we mean won't happen again?

3 How many times a year is the Empire State Building hit by lightning?

4 How does Ricky describe the idea of throwing a penny off a skyscraper?

5 Where do people demonstrate that water flushes differently in different halves of the world?

6 What determines the direction that water flushes down a toilet?

7 What can goldfish remember after three months?

8 What did fish have to press to get a reward in one experiment?

3 Listen again and complete the sentences.

1 It takes more than 10 percent of our brain to produce a _____ .
2 Roy Cleveland Sullivan was hit by lightning _____ .
3 Terminal velocity describes the _____ that a moving object can achieve.
4 Emily realises that people who charge to show tourists that water flushes differently in two hemispheres are playing _____ .
5 In an experiment, goldfish completed an action at _____ each day.
6 Ricky says that goldfish aren't as _____ as we thought they were.

4 🔊 **10.02 Listen to the next part of the podcast. Are the sentences true (T) or false (F)?**

1 Emily says that with certain myths, it's understandable why we believe them. ____
2 Ricky says that in some cases, we don't come across the correct information. ____
3 Ricky says there's no scientific evidence that humans contribute to global warming. ____
4 Ricky says that hearing something different to what we know causes anxiety. ____
5 Belief perseverance occurs when we change our ideas about something. ____
6 Ricky says that when we hear correct information, we recognise it as correct. ____

5 Match the words in bold with meanings a–f.

1 Scientists have proved that humans have an **impact** on global warming ____
2 Our mind doesn't seem to like **conflict** and so we avoid it. ____
3 So, how do we **justify** it to ourselves? ____
4 We choose to **misinterpret** the new information we receive. ____
5 We **dismiss** the information as being rubbish … ____
6 … or not from a **credible source**. ____

a refuse to consider
b a state of disagreement
c the effect someone/something has on someone/something
d a place that provides information which can be believed
e give an acceptable explanation for something
f not understand the correct meaning of facts you're considering

Reading

1 Read a letter that someone wrote to themselves as a teenager. What is the purpose of the letter?

a To predict the future

b To provide a warning not to do something

c To give some tips about life

2 Read the letter again. Match things 1–6 the writer talks about with topics a–f.

1 It happened quickly.

2 One day, I'll have the opposite opinion.

3 I worried about them.

4 I worried about it.

5 It wasn't enjoyable for me.

6 It's been life-changing.

a a job I had

b time in general

c having a family

d my appearance

e exams

f getting my first job

3 Are the sentences true (T) or false (F)?

1 The writer is unhappy about having a birthday. ....

2 The writer as a teenager doesn't want to be different to others. ....

3 The writer will keep in contact with all university friends. ....

4 The writer feels mature aged 25. ....

5 The writer feels that having an unenjoyable job was worth it. ....

6 The writer sometimes experiences sadness without any clear cause. ....

7 The writer said he had sufficient money to have children in his 30s. ....

8 The writer implied he had sufficient sleep when the children were young. ....

4 Which of these things can we infer from the letter?

1 The writer is sometimes forgetful.

2 The writer lacks confidence today.

3 The writer works too hard.

4 The writer enjoys taking risks in life.

5 The writer is sensible when it comes to money.

6 The writer's parents helped to look after his children.

5 Complete the pieces of advice with endings a or b.

1 The writer suggests participating in ....

a as many activities as possible while young.

b travel to different parts of the world.

2 The writer suggests spending more time ....

a working on projects you love.

b with friends and family.

3 The writer says that it's acceptable ....

a to have support when raising children.

b to start a family when you're young.

4 The writer believes that life is ....

a mostly easy.

b generally positive.

5 The writer says that the journey in life is more important than ....

a getting to where you want to go.

b being successful.

6 Find the words and phrases in the box in the letter. Match them with definitions 1–8.

loyal   made the most of
not a bed of roses   overall   perspective
rush   settle down   speed by

1 pass very quickly

....

2 considering or including everything

....

3 move very quickly

....

4 not a happy, comfortable or easy situation

....

5 the way of thinking about something

....

6 start living a quiet and calm life in one place

....

7 gained the greatest possible advantage from something

....

8 always supporting your friends

....

7 Complete the sentences with the correct form of the words and phrases in Exercise 6.

1 Now that I'm getting older, I'd like to

....

2 He thought it would be a .... , but it was really tough!

3 Don't .... to grow up; enjoy your childhood.

4 If you can't change the situation, then change your ....

5 Try to enjoy life and .... of every day.

6 Having .... friends is very important.

7 It's been a difficult six months but it's been worth it ....

8 The time just .... ; we were enjoying ourselves so much.

To my younger self,

Today, I turned 40. It's a milestone in life that no one can really prepare you for. One minute, you're 20, single and free. The next minute, 20 years have flown by and you're middle-aged with a wife and two daughters. Not that I'm complaining, it's just that life has a habit of speeding by. One thing that growing older gives you is perspective, so I wanted to look back on my life and give you some advice as you develop from a teenager to an adult.

You currently feel as if you're too tall and skinny. You round your shoulders to make yourself seem smaller so that you don't stand out. Don't do this. If people make fun of your height, ignore them. One day, you'll love how tall you are and how it draws attention to you. You'll feel good about who you are, both inside and out.

You'll do well in your exams despite feeling anxious about them. (Just remember to take your calculator to your maths exam because forgetting it will cause you more stress than is necessary.) You'll go to university and make amazing friends who'll recognise you for the generous, loyal person you are. You won't keep in touch with all of them after you leave, but you'll always remember them.

When you leave university, you still won't know exactly what you want to do with your life. Don't panic, that's OK. Not everyone has to jump immediately into a job. You'll decide to travel and while there, you'll have some incredible experiences. By the time you're 25, you'll have lived in three different countries and met your life partner. You'll feel like you're ready to settle down but looking back, you're still really young. Make sure you enjoy your 20s. Get out and do as much as you can. As you both get older, you'll start to do less and that's OK, but it helps when you know you made the most of your youth.

At the age of 30, you'll be working in a job you adore. It'll have taken you a bit of time to get there. You'll have spent a year working in a job that you hated, where the managers were cruel but the colleagues were kind. However, it'll prompt you to pursue a different career, the career of your dreams. Without experiencing unkind managers first, you won't take the risk so it's worth it in the end. One thing to note (and my current self should note this, too) is that life is a marathon and not a sprint. Don't feel as if you need to work 16 hours a day to get ahead. You can be successful and take time for yourself and the people you love, too.

As with your career, other aspects of your life will have their ups and downs. There'll be challenging times, like when you both decide you really want to start a family in your late 20s but realise you can't afford it yet. And then a few years later, when you are financially stable enough, the arrival of twins brings the realisation that you won't sleep for about three years. However, those babies will bring great joy and you'll love them like you've never loved anyone before. Just understand that it's fine to ask for help and be thankful they have grandparents.

So, life may not always be a bed of roses but it's been pretty good overall so far. Just don't rush to get to your destination. Make sure you enjoy the ride.

Yours lovingly,
Your older self

Writing

1 Read the article and put the advice in order 1–6.

a Choose the right time of day. ....

b Point the camera in the right direction.

....

c Get the lighting right. ....

d Position your mouth in the right way. ....

e Look at what's around you. ....

f Position the top part of your body in the right way. ....

2 Read the article again. Are the sentences true (T) or false (F)?

1 The article uses formal language. ....

2 The article sounds as if the writer's chatting to a friend. ....

3 The article tries to engage readers from the first line. ....

4 The article tries to inform the reader. ....

5 The article tries to paint a picture for the reader. ....

6 The article is divided into paragraphs based on topic. ....

How to take a successful selfie

Apparently, some of us spend between an hour and five hours a week taking selfies. This is an incredible number bearing in mind the fact that, before 2002, neither the word 'selfie', nor the concept really existed. So, how can we save ourselves time taking a hundred photos before getting that perfect one?

The first thing to consider is the setting. Keep it simple or make sure it's really interesting. Something in the middle might distract viewers but not in a good way. Beware of people pulling faces behind you or background objects that make you look as if you've got something strange growing out of your head.

Another thing to think about is the angle. Look up at the camera and you'll avoid looking like your double-chinned uncle. Try to hold the phone so that the bottom is level with your eyes. Holding it to the side rather than in front of you can be more flattering, too.

Move your head away from your neck and raise your eyebrows slightly, but remember that there's a fine line between having a long neck and wide eyes, and looking like a startled giraffe. Think about something happy, so your smile reaches your eyes. That way, it comes across as genuine. Pouting is great if you want to look like a duck, but it's not a very attractive look, regardless of what certain celebrities will have you believe. It's also a bit 2014.

The final thing to think about is lighting. Stand in sunlight or next to a window. Face the sun directly, or face directly away from it. Somewhere in between can cause nasty shadows which make you look tired. The best time of day for a selfie is at dawn when the sun is low.

So, set your alarm, get up nice and early, head outside, hold the camera the right way and smile. You won't regret it.

Attracting and keeping the reader's attention

Articles have to work hard to keep the reader's attention. There is a lot of competition and if the article is not interesting, the reader will quickly lose interest. For this reason, it's important to think about how to grab and keep the readers' attention.

- Don't be too formal.

The language that you might use in an essay (*on the one hand, what's more, to summarise*, etc.) is not appropriate for an article. Keep it more informal but not so informal that it sounds like you are writing a letter to a friend.

This is a vast number …   This is an incredible number …

- Think about your audience and don't state the obvious.

Say things that your audience would find interesting.

Try to smile.

Think about something happy, so your smile reaches your eyes.

- Write an interesting first line.

Use a quote, a controversial statement or a surprising fact to grab the reader's attention from the start. If you can't remember the quote exactly, use *Somebody once said …*

- Create interesting mental images.

Think about the pictures the reader sees in their mind when they read your article. The more interesting the mental images, the more the reader will enjoy the article.

… you'll avoid looking like your double-chinned uncle.

3 Read the Focus box. Then match article extracts 1–5 with purposes a–c.

1 Apparently, some of us spend between an hour and five hours a week taking selfies. ....

2 Try to hold the phone so that the bottom is level with your eyes. ....

3 ... looking like a startled giraffe ....

4 Pouting is great if you want to look like a duck. ....

5 Face the sun directly, or face directly away from it. ....

a Say things that your audience will find interesting

b Write an interesting first line

c Create interesting mental images

4 Complete the more informal sentences in the pairs with the words and phrases in the box.

afraid   far better   feel the need   find   help
long way   look like   time zones

1 Selfie apps can be beneficial. /
Selfie apps can be a great ....

2 Several attempts are acceptable. /
Don't be .... to keep trying.

3 Discover your best side. /
.... out what your most attractive side is.

4 Holding the camera high can result in a large forehead. /
If you hold the camera too high, your forehead might look like it's in two ....

5 Your equipment will contribute to the quality of the image. /
Your photo will look .... if you have the right equipment.

6 A photo editor will improve your photos. / A bit of editing can go a .... to improving your picture.

7 Artificial lighting is less flattering than natural light. /
Avoid artificial lighting that can make you .... Frankenstein's monster.

8 It's not necessary to look directly at the camera. /
Don't .... to look directly at the camera.

Prepare

5 Read the advertisement. Note down as many ideas for the article as possible, or write down ideas for your own 'tips' topic.

> How can we make sure we're polite when using a mobile phone in public?
>
> Write an article with your tips and we'll publish the best ones on our website.
>
> Email us at articles@phoneshop.uk

6 Plan your article. Use the following plan to help you.

Introduction: ....

Tip 1: ....

Tip 2: ....

Tip 3: ....

Tip 4: ....

Conclusion: ....

Write

7 Write your article. Check that it contains:

- an introduction and conclusion
- a main body divided into paragraphs
- an interesting first sentence
- informal language
- language which creates mental images
- ideas that an adult reader would find interesting

UNIT 1   Recording 1

P = Presenter   G = Graham

P: Joining me today is Graham Latimer who's recently written a book about our personalities. He says that every characteristic has its benefits, even the bad ones. So, Graham, why did you choose this topic?

G: Well, er … none of us are perfect. We all have characteristics that we think of as good and characteristics we think of as bad. But, you know, a lot of bad characteristics aren't actually bad at all.

P: Such as?

G: Well, let's take, um, laziness, for example. When someone's lazy, we imagine they … they lay around doing nothing. But what lazy people actually do is to make life easier for themselves. And this results in … in … inventions.

UNIT 1   Recording 2

P = Presenter   G = Graham

P: Joining me today is Graham Latimer who's recently written a book about our personalities. He says that every characteristic has its benefits, even the bad ones. So, Graham, why did you choose this topic?

G: Well, er … none of us are perfect. We all have characteristics that we think of as good and characteristics we think of as bad. But, you know, a lot of bad characteristics aren't actually bad at all.

P: Such as?

G: Well, let's take, um, laziness, for example. When someone's lazy, we imagine they … they lay around doing nothing. But what lazy people actually do is to make life easier for themselves. And this results in … in … inventions.

P: What do you mean?

G: Well, lazy people invent things to make their lives more comfortable. For instance, did you know that if you put your mobile phone in a glass, the sound is much louder?

P: Oh right, yeah, I've heard about that.

G: Yeah. And the likelihood is that a lazy person discovered it because, well, they didn't want to get up and find some speakers. See?

P: Ah, right. There's a saying, isn't there? That necessity is the mother of invention. So, what you're saying is that when you're a bit lazy, avoiding activity is a necessity and so lazy people invent things to avoid activity.

G: Exactly!

P: OK, now, I'm pretty messy – you should see my flat, there's stuff everywhere – and it's certainly something which my family see as a negative trait. Can you do me a favour and tell me that it's actually a positive thing?

G: Yeah, I can.

P: Great!

G: Research shows that messy people are … are … very creative people. They, er, also take more risks.

P: Oh, that's good. I can't wait to tell my family that!

G: We can say a similar thing about people who are easily bored. When … when we're bored, we actually spend time looking for … for new things to do or … looking for new knowledge to learn. We get creative.

P: Children use their imaginations when they're bored, don't they?

G: Yeah, they make their own games, but adults get creative, too, just perhaps in a different way. We try new things and imagine all kinds of possibilities that help us to, er, make better decisions.

P: That makes sense.

G: Optimism and pessimism are interesting characteristics. We … we think of optimism as being positive and pessimism as being negative, right?

P: Yeah.

G: Yeah, but actually pessimism is a positive characteristic.

P: Really? How come?

G: Well, when we're pessimistic, we always assume the worst. Something bad's always gonna happen, right? So, we prepare for it. That means, er, we take far fewer risks than people who are optimistic.

P: Right.

G: And the problem with optim … with … with being optimistic, is that it makes you think everything will work out and nothing bad will happen to you. So, of course, what that means is that you make no preparations for anything bad happening or avoid risks that a pessimistic person would avoid. The result of all this is that it's actually pessimistic people who live longer and healthier lives.

P: Really? That's fascinating.

G: It is. Not what most people would say at all.

P: No.

G: Um, another characteristic we think of as negative is shyness, but it isn't negative at all. Shy people may be reluctant to speak to new people, but are often … well, often make excellent listeners and they pay much more attention to what's around them than others. They can be excellent managers because, er, listening and observation skills are very important in that kind of job.

P: So, um, do you think that every negative characteristic is a positive?

G: Good question. Hmm, I'm not sure about every one, but I do think that the majority can be positive.

P: Interesting. Graham, thanks very much. It was great to hear your ideas today.

UNIT 2   Recording 1

A = Alicia   M = Marco

M: Hello and welcome to *My thoughts exactly* – the weekly podcast in which Alicia and I talk about … well, whatever we feel like, right?

A: Ha ha! Right.

M: I'm your host, Marco, and this week we're talking about complaining. Alicia, do you know anyone who complains?

A: Yeah, someone I used to work with. Let's call her Annie.

M: What did she moan about?

A: What didn't she moan about? The temperature of the office for one. It was always too cold for her. And then she complained if someone was late, even if they made up the hours at the end of the day. That used to really get on my nerves. And she hated it if someone brought smelly food in for lunch and ate at their desk, and then she …

M: Wait, wait stop!

A: What?

M: You're complaining! You're complaining, about someone complaining!

A: Oh yeah, I guess I am! But it's good to have a moan, isn't it? Complaining helps to get out your frustrations and makes you feel better.

M: Well, yes and no.

A: What do you mean?

M: Well, apparently, complaining about something to someone else can improve your mood slightly but not for long. In the end, it just makes you feel down.

A: Oh, right.

M: Yeah, I've read a bit of research about it. Complaining produces feelings of negativity. There was this one study where people were asked to write about their day, you know, every evening. Half the people were asked to write about positive things and the other half were asked to write about things that irritated them.

A: And?

M: Well, the half that complained about their day felt less satisfied that evening and were in a worse mood the next day, too.

A: Yeah, I can see how that happens.

M: Right. There's also a suggestion that complaining can have a physical effect on your body, too. It causes stress which, in turn, can do things like increase your blood pressure.

A: Oh, that doesn't sound good.

M: No, complaining makes the listener feel miserable, too, so, er, thanks for that!

A: Oops, sorry. So, it's a never-ending cycle. The complainer brings the listener down who, then spreads that misery around themselves!

M: Exactly, but I'll forgive you … this time!

A: Ha ha! Thanks. So, what do you suggest then? That we never complain about anything?

M: Of course not. I suppose the thing to do is, er, try to change what we're fed up about so we don't feel the need to moan.

A: So, if someone I know moans, I should talk to them about it.

M: Yeah, you should listen to the person and nod – because they probably just want some attention. It's tempting to start giving advice but complainers don't often want that.

A: That's true.

M: You could ask the person how they're gonna change the situation. That might focus their attention on finding a solution. Then take your own advice and think of positive things yourself! There are loads of studies that suggest that doing that helps you feel happier in general. Some people keep a gratitude diary.

A: What's that?

M: It's where you write about the things you're grateful for that day. You focus on the positive not the negative.

A: Oh, right.

M: It can help to change your mindset, or so people claim. For example, what three things did you like about Annie?

A: Hmm, well she could be pretty funny at times. And she often helped me when I didn't understand the software we used.

M: What else?

A: She made amazing cookies which she usually shared with me.

M: Lucky you! See? It's much nicer to be positive, isn't it?

A: I guess you're right. And if you can stop a moaner from moaning, too, then you'll both be content.

M: Hopefully!

UNIT 2   Recording 2

S1–8 = Speakers 1–8

S1: I know your boss can be really tough on you but don't let him bring you down.

S2: Stop being so negative all the time. Be more positive and change your mindset.

S3: I go home and moan about work for five minutes every day. It helps me to get rid of all my frustrations.

S4: Sorry I'm late – I promise I'll make the time up.

S5: It doesn't take much to make me happy. A hot bath, relaxing music and I'm content.

S6: You're such a complainer. All you do is moan!

S7: I'm so tired! I can't seem to focus today.

S8: There's a lot of negativity in here today. Why is everyone so miserable?

UNIT 3   Recording 1

S = Speaker

S: Thank you. So our memories are a huge part of us. We can even say that we are our memories. Memories give us a sense of our self-identity. They connect our past to our present and help to shape our future, but did you know that our memories are also unstable, unreliable and often inaccurate?

Our memories are incredibly complex and so little is known about how they work. We do know that a memory isn't one thing that sits in one area of our brain. It's created, stored and recalled using a complex set of systems across all parts of our brain which work together. So, if we think about an object that's important to us, we have a picture of it in our minds in one part of our brain, we have the emotions attached to that object in another part, and then there are the sounds and smells associated with it kept elsewhere. A memory brings all those things together from different parts of our brains.

But countless studies have shown that we can't rely on our memories to be accurate. For instance, we've all argued with a friend or a family member about the accuracy of a memory. You say an event took place in summer, while they say it was winter. Both of you believe 100 percent that you're correct because you're convinced your memory is reliable so the other person can't possibly be right. You remember clearly that the trees had green leaves on them and everyone took their jackets off because it was hot. Right?

Well, maybe not. Scientists now believe that a memory changes every time we recall it. This is because, every time we think about a memory or tell someone about it, we attach the emotions we have now to it. Our memories change according to who we are now. It could be, for example, that we want to impress someone so we slightly change the memory when we tell it to make us sound funnier, or more intelligent or braver. We probably don't even realise that we're doing it but next time we recall that memory, the new version is the one we remember. Let's imagine that we're annoyed with someone in our memory. When we recall the memory, we think of that person's action more negatively than before. The next time we recall it, those same negative feelings remain and the memory is changed. Again, we probably didn't even know how our emotions affected that memory. We think the memory's correct.

Whether or not these changes are permanent, we're not sure. Neuroscientists have, for a long time, assumed that after a short period of changes, our memories become stable. This is known as consolidation. Once a memory has been consolidated, it's assumed not to change as we age. However, this is now being questioned. One thing is for sure and that's the fact that there are still so many exciting things to learn about how our memory works that neuroscience is going to be an exciting industry to work in over the next few decades. Thank you.

UNIT 4   Recording 1

S = Sophie   M = Mara   J = James

S: Hey, James, have you seen this meme that Lewis has shared?

J: Yeah, it's really funny!

M: I haven't. I'm on a digital detox at the moment.

S: A digital what?

M: Detox … it means going offline for a month.

S: Oh, Mara! Why?

M: I don't know. I just waste so much time looking at pictures of other people's pets and babies. Babies I've never even met!

J: But what about work?

M: Yeah, I use the internet at work, obviously. I'm talking about when I'm at home.

S: Interesting … since when?

M: Last Thursday.

S: But you said you spent all weekend binge-watching a police drama!

M: Oh, yeah. OK, so it's just social media that I'm avoiding, not TV shows.

J: I don't think I could cope without social media! I'd feel like I was missing out.

M: I thought I would too but it turns out I quite like it. It's nice to be able to focus on something without getting distracted by messages. I've even started reading a book. First one in ages!

J: I know what you mean about the distractions. It can be hard to concentrate on something when your phone keeps buzzing. I can't stop myself looking though.

M: Well, our phones are designed that way, aren't they?

J: What do you mean?

M: Well, when we get a message, our body releases a chemical into our brains. It's called dopamine, I think. It makes us feel good. Designers make our phones buzz when a message arrives so we feel good and keep using our phone.

J: That sounds scary – like an addiction.

M: Well, it is in a way. Designers want us to form habits so we use their apps. It's why they include features like those three little dots that appear when someone's writing us a message.

S: How so?

M: They promise us some kind of reward – a message – and just the thought of that causes our brains to produce dopamine.

J: Wow! Now I know why I spend so much time staring at those dots!

M: Ha ha! Exactly! And while we wait, we feel both stressed and excited about what the message will be.

S: So, if we get a lift when we receive a message, does that mean we feel low when we don't get one?

M: Hmm, good question. I have no idea of the science but I know from experience that it's disappointing when the three dots appear and then disappear.

S: You're right!

M: I did read about an experiment where two groups of university students were asked to attend a lecture. One group had their phones in their bags. The other group left their phones and bags in another room. After a while, the researchers abandoned the experiment because the group without their phones were getting so anxious, the researchers thought it was endangering their mental well-being!

S: You're joking. I mean, I love my social media, but that's a bit extreme! I think I could manage an hour or two without my phone.

M: It's called separation anxiety. It's something more and more of us are suffering from.

S: Are we really so desperate to keep in touch with people?

M: Maybe. But some scientists think it's because our phones hold our digital memories, so if we lose our phone, it's like losing our own memory. That's what worries us.

S: Oh right, that kind of makes sense.

J: I did read about a new phobia – nomophobia. It's the fear of being without your phone. I guess it's the same as separation anxiety.

S: Well, I don't think I suffer from either and I want to prove it. I'm willing to go on a digital detox. James, do you want to give it a try?

J: No way. I'll support you though if you like!

UNIT 5   Recording 1

S = Speaker

S: Thank you. So, I was recently in Beijing for work and a Chinese colleague of mine took me to a well-known coffee shop chain. He ordered a coffee for himself and a tea for me because I don't speak Chinese. The shop assistant told us how much it was and I offered to pay. When my colleague explained that I would be paying in cash, the shop assistant stood there looking at me with her mouth open for a good ten seconds. It was like he'd told her I was the President of the United States or something. You see, Beijing is close to becoming a cashless society. It's a city where mobile phones and online payment systems are used for everything, including paying for shopping, train tickets and bills. There are other cities in China which aren't far behind Beijing, and other cities around the world which are aiming to be cashless in the near future. Sweden is probably the most advanced example with other Scandinavian countries close behind. There, many shops already refuse to accept cash and some banks don't work with cash either. Sweden could be cashless by 2023.

But is a cashless society actually desirable? Of course, we'd no longer have to worry about taking cash out of our account, which would save us time. Retailers wouldn't have to worry about keeping cash on their premises. Countries would no longer have to print money at great cost, leaving money for other things. It'd also be easier for us to pay by phone or card when we go abroad, rather than having to use a foreign currency. Of course, if technology failed, we'd be left without the ability to buy anything, and businesses would be unable to sell their goods and services. This could be a failure at your bank or simply the fact that your mobile phone's run out of battery.

Paying electronically is also difficult for people that don't have bank accounts. Homeless people or people who use the black market would also be left out. The gap between rich and poor might become even bigger. Elderly people who aren't very technical might also find it difficult to survive in a cashless society.

People who aren't very good at managing their money could also lose out. They might find that they spend more money when they pay by card than when they pay by cash. They might get into much more debt in a cashless society.

Crime is also an issue we'd need to consider. On the one hand, we wouldn't have to worry about people stealing our cash and the number of thefts would decrease significantly, but on the other hand, hackers could simply take money directly from our accounts. If they did, we'd have no other source of money.

So, what needs to happen for a cashless society to be possible? Well, firstly there needs to be an online payment system that banks and businesses can use. This system needs to be secure with few technical problems. Governments also need to make sure that no member of our society gets left behind. This might mean working with banks so that banks don't charge such people to have access to an account.

Just think. In ten years' time, we might not use any cash at all. That would mean children born then never actually see notes and coins except in a museum.

UNIT 6   Recording 1

P = Presenter   M = Mike   L = Lara

Podcast 1

P: ... let me give you an example. During an interview early in my career, I was asked what kind of salary I was expecting. I told them 'more than I was currently getting', which at the time wasn't a lot. So, that's what they did. They offered me just a bit over my existing salary. I was fine with that, until I discovered several months later that my colleague in exactly the same position as me was getting quite a lot more. Why? Because she'd asked for it. For many of us, discussing our salary when taking a new job and asking for a pay rise later on can be very uncomfortable. So, how can we make sure we get the pay we deserve? The first step is to get as much information as you can about what your job is worth in the job market, as well as the financial state of the company at the moment. Are their profits increasing or decreasing? This will help you to decide how much you think the company will be willing to pay you. It's also important not to just think about pay. There's lots of research that says job satisfaction isn't based on pay alone. Are there other benefits you could ask for instead, like a company car, health insurance or a gym membership?

Once you've decided what to ask for and what compromises you're willing to make when negotiating with the manager, gather evidence to support your request. Think about sales you've made or will make, projects you've done and so on. You might want to consider getting an alternative job offer. The company might be willing to pay more for you, if they think they might lose you to someone else.

Finally, you can present your idea in your job interview or when speaking to your boss about a pay rise. Be clear about what you'd like and why. Speak in a calm and friendly manner. Don't rush into making decisions. If your manager makes an offer, say that you'll think about it and get back to them if you're unsure. It's not a race. At some point, the negotiations will have to come to an end, even if the offer you received was disappointing. Make sure you thank them for listening, even if you're disappointed. This way, if you ever try to work for the company again in future, or if you remain at the company and try to negotiate again at some point, it'll be possible.

Podcast 2

M: Exactly! Anyway, I'm going to buy a new car next week but I'm dreading it.

P: Why?

M: I'm useless at agreeing on a price. I mean, I'm the type of person that ends up offering more than the asking price, not less! The whole process just makes me really uncomfortable.

P: I know what you mean. It is awkward, but my sister-in-law is amazing at this kind of thing and she taught me how to haggle. Do you want some tips?

M: Sure! No doubt some of our listeners will appreciate them, too.

P: Well, the first thing is to be friendly when talking to the salesperson. Start with some small talk and smile at them to create a bond. Don't start talking about the price too soon.

M: OK, so what should we talk about?

P: Well, start with the weather! And then ask questions about the car and let them speak, but don't let them push you into decisions too soon. If they try to do that, keep asking more questions. Let them know that it's you who's in control.

M: OK, so how do I raise the question of price, then?

P: Tell the salesperson that if they can drop the price then you'll be able to purchase the car today. Avoid asking them how much they can drop the price by as they won't actually tell you!

M: Makes sense. Now, one thing I hate is when they make an offer and I have to make a counter offer. I'm too embarrassed to go low so I end up dropping it just below their offer, so in the end I don't get much of a discount.

P: Yeah, that's pretty common. But remember that the salesperson deals with this kind of thing every day. They'll expect you to go low. They won't think the offer is stupid. It's a starting price, that's all.

M: OK. So, we then keep going back and forth with different offers.

P: That's right. Look the salesperson in the eye throughout the negotiation. Act confidently even if you don't feel it. You might also want to think about any extras you'd like that could be included in the price you pay. Things like different wheels, an entertainment system or insurance. Ask about those things as you get to the end of the negotiation – not at the beginning – then make sure the salesperson hasn't included them into the overall price.

M: That way, it's truly a good deal.

P: Exactly. And when you get a decent price, you'll feel really good that you got that and the extras.

M: Great. What if I start to panic and can't decide whether to accept the offer or not?

P: Tell them you've got a dentist's appointment or you have to take a work phone call or something. Say you'll be back in an hour or so. That way, you can take some time to think about the offer and talk it over with someone else.

M: That's great. OK, I'm feeling better about next week now. Although maybe you should come with me ...

UNIT 7 Recording 1

P = Presenter   S = Scott

P: OK, let's move on. Now, these days more and more people are giving up work in their 30s. Here to tell us how he managed to achieve such a feat is my next guest, Scott Bryson. Scott – welcome to the show.

S: Thanks for inviting me.

P: So, Scott. You've stopped working, right?

S: That's right. I don't have a nine-to-five job anymore. I gave that up a year ago and there are lots of others like me around the world. It's a movement called FIRE, which stands for 'financial independence, retire early'.

P: Can you explain what you mean by financial independence?

S: Sure. So, it means that you don't need to do a job in order to live. My partner and I are both 39 years old. We have two children but we don't have a mortgage. We also don't have any bank loans but we do have enough savings and investments to live on without needing an employer and a full-time job.

P: 39 is incredibly early to be financially independent. How did you manage it?

S: Well, we made a real effort to spend as little as possible over a long period of time. That sometimes meant making our own entertainment as a family, but it wasn't all that hard really. And we were able to save a lot of money over 15 years. We invested that money and that's what we can live off today.

P: So, what tips would you give someone who wants to be financially independent in the future?

S: Firstly, choose your home carefully. Don't live somewhere that's bigger than you need. That way you save on rent or a mortgage. Then, budget carefully for everything else. Don't spend more than you earn. I mean, I know that's obvious but it's hard for some people to do that.

P: It is.

S: And definitely no loans. So, no car loans or loans for a wedding. If you take out a mortgage, make sure it's as small as possible, with as low an interest rate as possible and then work hard to pay it off.

P: How much should people try to save?

S: Experts suggest 10–15 percent of your gross income, but as much as you can really. If you're really serious about becoming financially independent, you have to stop living just for today and plan for the future, too. That means no big, fancy meals out in restaurants or takeaways every week, no big, fancy cars with a car loan and no fancy holidays abroad. Cook your own meals as cheaply as you can – it's often healthier, too. Save meals out for special occasions and have staycations rather than big holidays.

P: You mean, stay at home instead of going somewhere on holiday?

S: Exactly! We stayed at home and took day trips so we didn't have to pay for accommodation. Or we took a tent, drove into the country and went camping. We could still enjoy life but with a view to enjoying the future, too.

P: Where should people put their savings?

S: Naturally, you need to find a bank account that'll offer you competitive interest rates but it's not enough to put your money in a bank, you need to invest it, too. If you're careful, you can earn an income outside your job.

P: OK, but it's easy to talk about saving money when you're part of a couple and you have two salaries. It also depends on how much you earn in the first place, doesn't it?

S: That's right. It takes some people longer than others to become financially independent and retire. It's not right for everyone, either.

P: What do you mean?

S: Well, for some people, when they become financially independent, they find life becomes more difficult, not easier. For me and my partner, we felt much happier when we were able to give up our full-time jobs and focus on projects we enjoyed. We both do some part-time work online and both love spending more time with the children. But for others, their work is a big part of their identity. They feel like they lose a big part of themselves when they give up that work – they don't have clear goals anymore and they lose contact with the people they work with. They can't spend all day with their friends because their friends are working, so as a result they feel lonely and a bit lost.

P: So, make sure it's really what you want before you do it.

S: Exactly! Some people enjoy working.

P: Well, it's been really interesting to hear your story and getting your advice, Scott. Thank you very much.

S: My pleasure.

UNIT 7 Recording 2

A = Annie   M = Mark   L = Lisa

M: Shall we move onto this year's street party then, Annie?

A: Yes, let's do that.

M: So, when are we planning to have it?

A: It's usually the last weekend in May, isn't it, Lisa?

L: That's right.

A: I don't see any reason to change it.

L: Neither do I. Last year there was a problem with the location. Some new residents in Hill Street complained that the road was closed and they couldn't get out of their houses.

A: Yes, well, we did put up posters warning everyone it'd be closed.

M: I think they'll be more aware of it this year but to be on the safe side, let's put a note through everyone's door in the street.

L: Good idea. Hill Street's the best location. Can you make a note of that, please, Mark?

M: Yep. Er, what about guests. Who can come?

L: I think that anyone who lives in the village can come. We usually get about 75 people, don't we?

M: Yeah. I just wondered if we wanted to open it up to residents in nearby villages.

A: Hmm, I'm not sure about that. I think it's big enough already. What do you think Lisa?

L: I agree with you.

M: OK, and how much should we charge everyone?

L: I think we should put the price up to £10 per person this year. Everything's going to cost a bit more.

A: Hmm, I'm not sure. Can we put a question mark by that and leave it for another meeting?

M: Of course.

L: Are we going to borrow tables and chairs from the village hall again this year?

A: Yeah, and we'll ask people that live in the street to bring their own if we need more. Last year we asked three cafés in town to provide food. We paid them, but we got a huge discount in exchange for free advertising. I'm not sure it was successful. I'd like to get your views on that.

L: I agree. They just didn't provide enough. I think we should go back to what we did originally and ask people to bring food and drink to share.

M: I agree, but why don't we do both?

L: Actually, that's a good idea. Then we'll have plenty for everyone.

A: Good. I'll speak to the cafés. Right, that just leaves us with the entertainment then. Same DJ as last year?

M: Actually, my cousin's just started up as a DJ. He said he'll do the event for free.

A: Really? Is he any good?

M: Yeah, he's pretty good. He's got all his own equipment and a licence.

A: That's great! Get him booked!

M: Will do.

L: I'll speak to the police about getting the right paperwork so we can apply for permission to close the road again.

A: Great, shall we meet again this time next week to complete that paperwork? We can also talk about advertising.

M: Sure. And the price of tickets, too.

L: Great!

S1–6 = Speakers 1–6

S1: We need to get a plumber out to fix the taps in the toilets on the first floor, second floor and so on. They all need fixing.

S2: So, we've decided to increase the number of invitations to approximately 30.

S3: We need to do some research so that we have more information about the area.

S4: Ken will hire a minibus and everyone else can go with him.

S5: The recent storm lead to a power cut in three villages.

S6: Dan should call Sally about the DJ. She can book someone if necessary.

B = Ben   L = Lynne

B: Right, let's make a plan for our trip, then.

L: Yep, let me get a pen to make a list. OK, go.

B: Well, the flight leaves at six in the morning so we'll have to drive to the airport and park there.

L: OK, I'll do some research online and find a cheaper car park than last year. The price there has gone up by about 50 percent!

B: Really? Unbelievable. OK, good, you sort that out then.

L: No problem.

B: I'll speak to Ed next door about looking after the house while we're gone. You know, water the plants, feed the cat and so on.

L: Tell him that we'll buy him something nice from Spain as a thank you!

B: Will do. Write that down so we don't forget!

L: I'm writing it now.

B: What about packing?

L: Well, the kids can pack their own cases. They're old enough now.

B: Really? You trust them?

L: Ha! We can check they've got what they need.

B: OK. We need to buy a new suitcase. Do you remember one broke last year?

L: Oh, yeah. OK, I'll do that online. I'll make sure I get one with four wheels, too. They're much better.

B: Let's not forget sun cream.

L: No, I'll get a small bottle from the chemist's in town at the weekend. We can buy more during the week from the hotel shop.

B: It'll be more expensive.

L: I don't mind. It'll be easier than carrying it.

B: Fine. I'll check that we've still got travel insurance. I'll get some more if necessary.

L: Oh yeah, I forgot about that. Well remembered!

B: Thanks!

L: I'll get the passports out and put them in the case so we don't go without them.

B: What about entertainment?

L: What about it?

B: What will we let the kids take?

L: They can take their tablets. They can download some music, films and stuff onto those.

B: I'll download some books for me onto my phone.

L: And I'll be old-fashioned and buy a couple of books at the airport!

B: We should take some games, too. The kids like playing games in the evenings, especially cards.

L: Good idea. Right, I can't think of anything else, can you?

B: No, I think that's it for now. Oh, money! We need some euros.

L: Oh wow, we're hopeless, aren't we? OK, I'll order those online and I'll pick them up from the bank on Friday. I'll get approximately 500 euros. We can use our debit cards, too.

B: Great!

L = Luke   S = Sofia

S: Hey, look at that over there. What a mess!

L: It's art, isn't it?

S: You call that art, Luke? Hardly!

L: It is!

S: It's just mindless graffiti. That's not art. It's ugly.

L: Art doesn't have to be pretty, Sofia. Maybe the quality isn't very good, but it's still art.

S: You and I obviously have a different view of what art is!

L: For me, it's about creative freedom. Anything that someone has the freedom to create is art.

S: So, if I draw a stick man on this napkin here, that's art.

L: Of course!

S: So all graffiti is art to you, even when it's just people spray painting their names.

L: Well, as I said before, while some graffiti is better than others, it's still art because that person expressed themselves through their name.

S: Would you want it sprayed on your wall at home?

L: No, of course not, but there are some famous works of art I wouldn't want in my house either!

S: We agree on that then!

L: But, may I remind you that graffiti has been around since the beginning of humanity. Cave paintings, political graffiti on Roman buildings … people like to express themselves.

S: But people in caves didn't just write their names! They at least drew pictures that represented their lives.

L: That's only because they didn't have written language then. I'm sure if they had, they'd have made political statements.

S: And scrawled their names everywhere?

L: Probably!

S: I think the key issue for me is that graffiti's against the law. I appreciate that some artists take risks to express themselves and some street art can make a place look more attractive or, at the very least, more interesting. But the fact is that graffiti is still very much illegal and a lot of it is a waste of time.

L: I hear what you're saying and I do understand your point. I'm not one of those people who are interested in street art just because it brings more colour into a place and stops it from looking miserable. No, what I love is seeing art that's both imaginative and clever. I mean, I saw something the other day that made me laugh. There was a wall with a bush growing over the top of it. Someone had drawn the face of a woman underneath it so the bush looked like her hair. It was witty and I loved it. You just couldn't get that same effect in a gallery – it wouldn't work.

S: That does sound fun and also something that I'd call art. You know, I think what I'd like to see is more legal places where artists can create art. That way, we'd encourage more of the good stuff.

L: OK, yeah, but I doubt the wall that the artist painted that woman on was legal. If artists can only paint on buildings that are legal, their creativity would be reduced. There's no freedom there.

S: Well, what about the freedom of building owners? The people that actually own that wall? They now have to decide whether to clean it off or keep it. Why should they have to do either? Where's their freedom to own a wall without someone painting on it?

L: Tell that to people who owned buildings where Banksy created works of art. They're worth millions now.

S: That doesn't make it better. It probably makes it even worse because you have people coming to stare at it or even trying to steal it. I read somewhere that it can cost thousands to get security people in to look after it.

L: Hmm, I can definitely see your point. I'd never really thought of it from the owners' point of view and I'm not sure all street artists do either.

S: Freedom is one thing, but freedom comes with responsibility and an artist needs to take that responsibility seriously. We all live together and need to work together to keep the areas we live in safe and comfortable for everyone. That means we might have to compromise.

A = Abi

A: So, you wanna be famous? Well, it's never been easier to get your name and face out there for everyone to see. Here are my top five tips for becoming a celebrity.

One. Go on a reality TV show. While you're there, make sure you stand out. Even if it's for all the wrong reasons, people will pay attention to you. When they do that, you'll start appearing in the newspapers and the job offers will start rolling in. Just make sure that you put the work in so that people take you seriously and want to keep working with you. No one wants to work with a constant attention-seeker.

Two. Post a YouTube video that everyone will talk about. Do something silly, do something funny or do something clever. It doesn't matter, as long as people share it so it goes viral. Just take care not to make something that looks too fake – it should be as authentic as possible or people will notice. Release the video early in the week, as people are more likely to watch it at work before their week gets busy. Share it with all your friends, too, and hope that they pass it on.

Three. Become a social media influencer. Choose something that interests you and post photos on that topic. But be specific. Don't just post photos of food or clothes, post photos of, for example, vegan food or 80s clothes you can wear today. Think of what will make you different from the rest. Post regularly, chat with your followers and choose your hashtags carefully. You want people to be able to find out about you. Once you become well-known, you'll be sent free stuff and asked to advertise products for money. Then you can give up your day job.

Four. Start an argument with someone famous online. People love a good social media argument, but it's risky. Choose your words carefully, of course. No one wants to hear you insulting their favourite artist, but you can complain about a topic without being rude. The louder you shout, the more you'll be heard. Just choose the person carefully. Some stars have fans that would die for them. Pick someone whose fans are less passionate though, or you'll be receiving hate mail for months.

Five. This one will take much more work, but you could develop a skill and use it to become famous. It'll take much longer but you could become a professional athlete or a musician and make a name for yourself that way. Or you could invent something new – a product or an idea that will change the world. When Mark Zuckerberg first came up with the idea for Facebook, he had no idea it'd change the way we live our lives. Perhaps you could create a new app that will change everything? That will surely bring in both money and satisfaction.

R = Ricky   Z = Zoe

R: So, in this week's episode, I thought we'd deal with those science facts that we all know and love but which might not actually be true at all.
Z: Like what?
R: Well, I thought I'd test you.
Z: OK.
R: So, I'm going to give you some science 'facts' and you can tell me whether you think they're true or not. Sound good?
Z: Yeah, let's do it.
R: Right. The first one is that we – humans – only use 10 percent of our brains.
Z: Ah, OK. Well, I think that one's true, isn't it? We haven't really learnt how to fully use our brains yet.
R: Nope, sorry. It's fiction I'm afraid.
Z: Oh, right. So, what percentage of our brains do we use then?
R: We use all of it.
Z: Oh.
R: Yeah. We might not be using all of it every minute of the day, but we know from brain scans that there's no part that we don't use. Even just saying a sentence uses greater than 10 percent of our brains.
Z: OK, well that was a good start then! What's the next one?
R: Lightning doesn't strike twice.
Z: Ooo! I know this one. It's fiction, isn't it? There's some poor guy who got hit by lightning seven times or something.

R: That's right. Roy Cleveland Sullivan. He survived every one of them.
Z: Incredible.
R: We use the saying 'lightning never strikes twice' when we want to say that something bad won't happen to a person again, but, in reality, lightning can strike the same object many times – or person, as the rather unlucky Mr Sullivan discovered. The Empire State Building in New York gets hit around a hundred times a year.
Z: Wow!
R: Speaking of the Empire State Building, here's my next 'fact'. If you dropped a penny from the top of the Empire State Building, it would seriously injure a person on the ground.
Z: Hmm, yeah, I've heard this before. I thought it was true but now I'm not so sure. I'm gonna say it's fiction.
R: And you're right. People think that the penny would travel at such a speed that it'd do real damage to someone but in fact, it'd hit what we call terminal velocity. That's the maximum speed that any object travels at. Getting hit by a penny at terminal velocity would hurt, so throwing pennies off a tall building is a silly idea. But it wouldn't do serious harm to anyone.
Z: Good to know!
R: Right, next. Toilets flush in different directions in the northern hemisphere compared to the southern hemisphere.
Z: Hmm, I think this is fiction, although I've heard it's true, too. When you go to the Equator, people show you how the water goes round in one direction on one side of the Equator, and then in the other direction on the other side.
R: Yeah, but the direction your toilet flushes depends on the shape of your toilet and not the hemisphere. So, those people showing you are simply using one bowl in the northern hemisphere and another bowl, with a slightly different shape, in the south.
Z: Oh right. They charge for it, too! So, it's a trick, then!
R: Yeah, seems to be. OK, you've got two out of four so far. Let's see if you can get the last one. Goldfish have a memory that lasts three seconds.
Z: Hmm, well you haven't given me a fact yet so I'm going to say this one's true.
R: No, sorry! Experiments have shown that goldfish can learn survival tricks and remember them several months later. In one experiment, the fish had to push a handle to get some food. Not only did they remember to do it for several months during the experiment, they learnt to do it at the same time each day. They might not have the biggest attention spans but they're also not quite as forgetful as we think they are.

R = Ricky   Z = Zoe

Z: So, why do we believe this stuff then? I mean, with some things it's clear. We all want to believe that there are more things we can do with our brains than we can now. It's exciting to think there's more to discover. But what about the other myths?
R: Well, it might just be that you've seen it online or someone has told you about it, and you've never actually seen anything to contradict it.
Z: Right.
R: But there are some things that people believe despite lots of evidence telling them it's not true. Like our impact on global warming, for example. Scientists have proved that humans have an impact on global temperatures but there are still people who don't believe it.
Z: Why?
R: It might be due to a phenomenon called 'belief perseverance'. It's where people find it stressful to change a belief they have so they continue to believe it.
Z: Why do they find it stressful?
R: Our mind doesn't seem to like conflict and so we avoid it. It's just much easier to keep believing something we've always believed than to change our minds.
Z: Even when there's plenty of evidence otherwise?
R: Exactly.
Z: So, how do we justify it to ourselves?
R: We choose to misinterpret the new information we receive, or we dismiss it as being rubbish or not from a credible source.
Z: Interesting. So, I could dismiss everything you've told me today and continue to believe these science myths.
R: You could, but I wouldn't recommend it!

ANSWER KEY

UNIT 1

1A

1
1 c 2 a 3 f 4 b 5 e 6 h 7 d 8 g
2
1 relied on 2 deal with 3 work on 4 smile at
5 thinking about/of 6 suffer from 7 stand for
3
1 Who put these books here?
2 Do you know what time the film starts?
3 Who are you looking at?
4 Do you belong to any clubs?
5 Could I ask how old you are?
6 I wonder why nobody's here yet.
7 Who called you so early this morning?
8 I'd love to know where Tom gets his energy from.
4
1 d 2 g 3 c 4 e 5 a 6 f 7 h 8 b
5
1 what time the shops (usually) close
2 does BBC stand for
3 gave you that necklace
4 what Sam's doing/where Sam is
5 project are you working on
6 why Matt was rude to me yesterday
7 happened after the meal last night
8 how many countries Anna has visited

1B

1
1 b 2 c 3 e 4 f 5 g 6 h 7 d 8 a
2
1 big impact 2 bawled my eyes out 3 in shock
4 feel ashamed 5 inspired me 6 a total fool
7 believe her luck 8 blew my mind
3
1 was waiting, saw 2 used to
3 was coming down, was getting 4 kept
5 'd go 6 beating
4
... the head teacher ~~was often giving me~~
often gave/**would often give** me extra
responsibilities.
... , I ~~was doing~~ **did** something really silly.
... , ~~were~~ waiting for the teacher
... so we ~~were deciding~~ **decided** to take ...
I ~~would feel~~ **felt** very ashamed ...
I ~~was never forgetting~~ **forgot** ...
5
1 While I was sitting outside this morning, I saw a
really unusual looking bird.
2 Although Maddie took loads of driving lessons
last year, she failed her test.
3 André used to work at the local bank but now
he has his own business.
4 We looked/were looking at the menu, trying to
decide what to eat.
5 My family and I would often go/often used to
go camping in the summer holidays.
6 I once broke a finger while I was playing
basketball.

1C

1
1 outgoing 2 cautious 3 reserved
4 adventurous 5 trusting 6 organised
7 confident 8 suspicious

2
1 cautious 2 careless 3 trusting
4 adventurous 5 reserved 6 outgoing
7 suspicious 8 organised
3
1 a 2 e 3 c 4 f 5 d 6 b
4
1 c 2 a 3 b 4 c 5 a 6 a
5
1 This article doesn't make sense.
2 You'll have to wait in line to get the tickets.
3 None of my colleagues take an interest in my
work.
4 If we don't meet our deadline, we'll be in trouble.
5 If you feed our cat while we're away, I'll return
the favour when you next go away.

1D

1
1 c 2 a 3 b 4 c 5 c 6 b
2
1 What makes you say that?
2 I'm not really with you on that one. /
I'm really not with you on that one.
3 Can you explain that a bit more?
4 You might be right, I guess.
5 That happened to me once.
6 How did you come to that conclusion?
7 You could look at it another way.
8 That reminds me of the time I went to Spain.
3
1 You're absolutely right.
2 What makes you say that?
3 Are you serious?
4 You've got a point
5 In my experience
6 How did you come to that conclusion?
4
1 options 2 main/obvious
3 drawback/disadvantage 4 against
5 option 6 benefit/advantage
7 account/consideration 8 balance

Reading

1
1 Descriptive article
2
1 c 2 b 3 a 4 b 5 a 6 c
3
1 traditional offline dating is dead
2 much more time
3 introduce a new topic
4
1 tell (something)
2 converse with
3 fall into easy conversation
4 hit if off (with someone)
5 make judgements (about someone)
6 make a good impression
7 put someone at ease
8 be relieved
5
1 impression 2 off 3 easy conversation
4 tell 5 with 6 make

Listening

1
b
2
1 optimism 2 pessimism 3 laziness
4 shyness 5 messiness 6 boredom
3
1 d 2 f 3 b 4 e 5 a 6 c

4
1 inventions 2 risks 3 creative 4 prepare
5 attention 6 leaders

Writing

1
3 A place that surprised me
2
1 F *The writer says it's places that we have no
expectations of that are surprising.*
2 F *The writer arrived early to avoid crowds.*
3 T
4 T
5 F *It was bigger than the writer imagined.*
6 T
3
1 a 2 e 3 d 4 b 5 c 6 f 7 g
4
1 c 2 d 3 b 4 f 5 a 6 e
5
The floor in the hotel lobby; *like*
6
1 d 2 c 3 a 4 b
7–11
Students' own answers.

UNIT 2

2A

1
1 rest 2 rid of 3 attention 4 nerves
5 together 6 paid 7 straight 8 it
2
1 get in touch with 2 get carried away
3 get to see 4 get the feeling
5 getting on my nerves 6 get rid of
7 get his attention 8 get some rest
3
1 a 2 a 3 b 4 a 5 b 6 b 7 a 8 b
4
1 's/has been uploading 2 's/has uploaded
3 has become 4 have seen
5 's/has gained 6 's/has earned
7 have been supporting

2B

1
Across: 1 action 3 a law 5 funding
6 research
Down: 2 the dangers 3 a problem
4 alternatives
2
1 ban 2 enforce 3 crack 4 carried
5 do 6 warn 7 tackle 8 increases
3
1 take action 2 offer alternatives
3 tackle the problem
4 warn (their children) about the dangers
5 enforce a law 6 do more
4
1 being built 2 was hit 3 had been
4 be given 5 get 6 sent 7 speak
8 be given
5
1 are being given/have been given 2 organises
3 was started 4 have been invited
5 are trained 6 are also offered
7 have been given 8 receive 9 be given
10 get

2c

1
1 cold caller 2 faulty product
3 slow delivery 4 aggressive salesperson
5 false advertising 6 billing dispute
7 lack of communication 8 broken promise

2
1 c 2 a 3 b 4 a 5 b 6 c 7 c 8 a

3
1 frustrating 2 correct 3 inspiring
4 alarmed 5 convinced 6 tempting

4
1 A 2 B 3 B 4 A 5 B 6 A

5
1 confusing 2 satisfying 3 astonished
4 tempted 5 entertaining 6 exhausted

Listening

1
c

2
1 smelly food 2 your mood 3 irritated
4 satisfied 5 blood pressure 6 listener
7 nod 8 situation 9 grateful 10 cookies

3
1 moaned 2 made up 3 frustrations
4 negativity 5 down 6 focus 7 mindset
8 content

4
1 make up 2 bring someone down
3 frustrations 4 focus your attention on
5 moan 6 content 7 negativity
8 change your mindset

5
1 down 2 mindset 3 frustrations 4 up
5 content 6 moan 7 focus 8 negativity

Reading

1
c

2
1 Paragraph 3 2 Paragraph 1
3 Paragraphs 4 and 5 4 Paragraph 1
5 Paragraph 5 6 Paragraph 4 7 Paragraph 4
8 Paragraph 2

3
1 perform successfully
2 behave more positively
3 under the speed limit 4 physical energy
5 loyal 6 posts 7 education 8 support
9 applied effectively 10 at the top

4
1 concept 2 popping up 3 well-being
4 at random 5 promote
6 a win-win (situation) 7 transformed
8 demotivate 9 ineffective 10 context

5
1 well-being 2 contexts
3 a win-win situation 4 demotivated
5 ineffective 6 promote 7 at random
8 transform 9 pop up 10 concept

6
2, 3, 5

Writing

1
Both

2
1 He's been busy with work.
2 He got a promotion at work.
3 He's working a lot on some big projects.
4 It's challenging, interesting and well-paid.
5 His salary wasn't high enough.
6 A new house closer to work.

3
Asking for news: 3
Giving news: 1, 2

4
1 I'm really sorry to hear about your aunt.
2 Great news about your job.
3 How's it going at work?
4 I'm really pleased to hear about your exam results.
5 Have you heard about Kate?
6 What have you been doing recently?
7 As for me, I've taken up a new hobby.
8 I'm so sorry about your cat.

5
Asking for news: 3, 5, 6
Giving news: 7
Reacting to bad news: 1, 8
Reacting to good news: 2, 4

6
1 have you been doing recently?
2 really/so sorry (to hear) (the news) about your neighbour.
3 you heard the news about William?
4 really pleased (to hear) about your engagement.
5 's it going (over there) in the big city?
6 so/really sorry (to hear) about your (broken) leg.
7 been busy with football (recently).
8 like you're enjoying yourself on holiday.

7
1 b 2 a 3 b 4 b

8–10
Students' own answers.

UNIT 3

3A

1
1 'd stopped 2 bought 3 been watching
4 had been shining 5 'd never 6 'd been
7 ordered 8 had been working

2
1 had bought 2 had been raining
3 had been riding/had ridden
4 'd/had just made 5 'd/had been baking
6 had made 7 had sent 8 had already moved
9 had never met 10 had been

3
1 memory 2 reminds 3 memorise 4 recall
5 memory 6 memorable 7 mind 8 forget

4
1 Can/Do you recall the name
2 Does this music remind you of anything?
3 that meeting was memorable
4 I've always had a good memory for numbers
5 I'll never forget the time
6 I have/'ve got no memory of it at all
7 None of us need to memorise history dates

3B

1
1 arrogant 2 inexperienced 3 thoughtful
4 remarkable 5 tough 6 unpredictable
7 confident 8 determined

2
1 stubborn 2 bold 3 competitive
4 thoughtful 5 reasonable 6 determined
7 remarkable 8 arrogant

3
1 a lot 2 more 3 as 4 by far 5 as warm
6 less 7 least 8 much more

4
1 far 2 than 3 the 4 more 5 a
6 much 7 The 8 as

5
1 as good/as 2 was more/than
3 far the fastest 4 isn't as nice as
5 lot less/than 6 The more tired/the less
7 too tired 8 play as well as

3c

1
1 h 2 b 3 a 4 f 5 d 6 e 7 g 8 c

2
1 b 2 e 3 c 4 a 5 d 6 g 7 f

3
-al: ethical, historical, logical
-ful: colourful, useful
-ic: allergic, historic
-ish: foolish, nightmarish
-less: colourless, pointless, useless
-ous: outrageous, ridiculous
-able/ -ible: acceptable, adaptable
-y: meaty, scary

4
1 doable 2 tricky 3 traditional 4 classic
5 likeable 6 poisonous 7 respectful
8 confidential

5
1 apologetic 2 reasonable 3 delightful
4 accidental 5 sensible 6 disrespectful
7 pointless 8 nightmarish

3D

1
1 bread 2 fruit juice 3 cheese
4 cauliflower 5 tomatoes

2
1 raw 2 filling 3 tough 4 creamy
5 greasy 6 bland 7 salty 8 crunchy

3
1 We have/need to be somewhere in 15 minutes.
2 Is this soup supposed to be cold?
3 I asked for chips but (I've) got mashed potato.
4 Could/Can you check on the/our order for me (please)?
5 This steak is (a bit/very/really/too) tough. / Could/Can I speak to the manager?

4
1 The service gets a big thumbs up.
2 Your cakes are one of your strong points.
3 Perhaps you could bear the feedback in mind.
4 Your staff might want to try being a bit more polite.
5 Overall, people felt that the food was good.
6 I'll take that on board.

5
1 d 2 b 3 h 4 a 5 g 6 c 7 f 8 e

Reading

1
b

2
1 T
2 T
3 F *We might respect them.*
4 F *It increases it.*
5 T
6 F *We might focus only on our rival and miss the other competitors.*

3
1 Paragraph 3 2 Paragraph 2 3 Paragraph 4
4 Paragraph 1 5 Paragraph 6 6 Paragraph 3
7 Paragraph 1 8 Paragraph 4 9 Paragraph 2
10 Paragraph 5 11 Paragraph 6
12 Paragraph 5

4
1 reject 2 revealing
3 decide to act in a particular way

5
1 drive someone to do something 2 challenge
3 strength 4 weakness 5 innovative
6 cheat 7 motivated 8 dominate

6
1 weaknesses 2 cheating 3 to challenge
4 has dominated 5 strengths 6 innovative
7 motivated

7
1 higher 2 continued 3 necessary
4 significantly 5 high 6 hard

Listening
1
a
2
1 c 2 b 3 a 4 b 5 a 6 c
3
Sentence 3

Writing
1
a
2
1 not so long ago 2 for about two stops
3 all of a sudden 4 in the end
5 After a few minutes 6 In the meantime
3
1 in 2019, nowadays
2 after a few hours, the following day, over time
3 in the meantime, meanwhile
4 all of a sudden, as soon as, eventually
4
1 over time 2 eventually 3 in early 2016
4 as soon as 5 in the meantime 6 Nowadays
7 After hours 8 The following day
5
1 in late 2014 2 All of a sudden
3 In the meantime 4 eventually
5 as soon as 6 nowadays
6–8
Students' own answers.

 UNIT 4

 4A

1
1 flimsy 2 chunky 3 oval 4 sparkly
5 rectangular 6 designer 7 priceless
8 identical
2
1 priceless 2 decorative 3 elegant
4 vivid-pink 5 sparkly 6 designer
7 oval 8 chunky 9 identical
3
1 You need a big, chunky necklace with that dress.
2 I hate these cheap, flimsy bedsheets.
3 Have you got any of those small, plastic plates?
4 I've never seen a watch with such a huge, round face!
5 Manu only ever wears designer cotton shirts.
6 Those are very elegant, gold earrings.
4
1 I really enjoyed that book on psychology which/that you lent me.
2 My parents, who now live in Spain, are both retired.
3 I met a woman who works with you today.
4 The museum (which) you're talking about is called The Williamson.
5 My phone, which I only got last year, isn't working.
6 I helped a man whose car had broken down last night.
5
1 That's the bus driver who I had an argument with/with whom I had an argument this morning.
2 Susanne, whose children go to school with mine, is a doctor.
3 The restaurant's in Gold Street, which is in the east of the city.
4 William's sister Jenny, who works in marketing, has just got a big promotion.
5 I'm so sorry but I left the umbrella you lent me on the metro.
6 My flat, which overlooks the park, is in a pretty nice area of the town.

6
1 c who 2 a which 3 e which
4 d which/that 5 g which/that
6 b which/that 7 f whose

 4B

1
1 c 2 f 3 a 4 d 5 b 6 e
2
1 have a flair for 2 have a passion for
3 have/get a degree in 4 experience in
5 have critical thinking skills 6 cope with
7 Are you willing to 8 'm not bothered about
3
1 to 2 were 3 had/needed 4 has/needs
5 didn't 6 weren't 7 got 8 must
9 have/need
4
1 correct
2 You can't/aren't allowed to/mustn't eat in here.
3 Jamie had to go to the next meeting but I didn't have to. / Jamie's got to go to the next meeting but I don't have to.
4 correct
5 We weren't allowed to stay up late when we were kids.
6 correct
7 You don't have/need to call me tomorrow but you can if you want.
8 Alison didn't have to go to work yesterday. / Alison doesn't have to go to work today.
5
1 We have to get up early tomorrow.
2 I wasn't allowed to go out alone at night when I was a child.
3 Sara wasn't required to go into work early, but she did anyway.
4 You (really) must see a dentist about your tooth.
5 You can't bring your own food into the cinema.
6 David doesn't need to come to the meeting.
7 You've got to pay more attention to me when I'm speaking!
8 You really didn't have to bring me a present.

 4C

1
1 selfie 2 google 3 emojis/emoticons
4 meme 5 contactless 6 unfriend
2
1 virtual assistant 2 binge-watching
3 crowdsource 4 time-poor 5 hashtag
6 paywall
3
1 c 2 a 3 c 4 b 5 b 6 a
4
1 brightens 2 shorten 3 saddens 4 soften
5 enlarge 6 enforce
5
1 lessening 2 broaden 3 enrich 4 shorten
5 endanger 6 ensure

Listening
1
All except for Ways of using social media and Trying a new app
2
1 T
2 F *She's off social media only.*
3 F *He can't stop himself from looking.*
4 F *When we receive a message.*
5 T
6 F *He always does.*
7 T
8 F *It describes being afraid of having no mobile phone.*

3
1 (Other people's) Pets
2 A (police) drama
3 social media
4 Reading a book
5 Concentrate (on something)
6 An addiction
7 Stressed and excited
8 Our (own) memory
4
1 d 2 f 3 b 4 a 5 e 6 c
5
1 Sophie 2 James 3 Mara 4 Mara
5 James

Reading
1
1 b 2 d 3 a 4 f 5 e 6 c
2
1 b 2 a 3 c 4 a 5 b
3
1 dramatically 2 constantly 3 impact
4 struggle 5 mental well-being 6 confidence
7 natural resources 8 transporting
4
Sentence 2
5
1 Catty86, Linz99 2 Vichan, Linz99
3 AdLib3, Hannah 4 Catty86 5 Vichan
6 Hannah 7 Linz99 8 Catty86
6
1 motivates 2 donate 3 tell 4 tick off
5 reminder

Writing
1
Repair technician
2
1 d 2 a 3 c 4 b
3
1 I have very strong active listening skills.
2 I would be happy to attend an interview at any time.
3 I feel I would be a great asset to your company.
4 More recently I worked for a media company. / I more recently worked for a media company.
5 I've worked as a social media manager where I was tasked with monitoring social media.
6 I believe I am the perfect fit for your company because of my brand knowledge.
4
1 attention to detail
2 patience
3 a creative flair
4 an ability to show care and empathy for people's treasured possessions
5 determination/an ability to solve challenging problems
5
1 others 2 ideas 3 support 4 information
5 oriented 6 adapt
6–8
Students' own answers.

UNIT 5

 5A

1
1 stock up 2 set aside 3 pay back
4 cut back on 5 take out 6 splash out (on)
7 live on 8 get into debt
2
1 splashed 2 goes 3 take/get 4 cut
5 live 6 got 7 stock 8 set
3
1 e 2 b 3 a 4 f 5 d 6 c 7 g
4
1 have bothered 2 was supposed to
3 have had 4 shouldn't 5 go 6 be 7 'd

5
1 hadn't forgotten 2 hadn't eaten 3 to get
4 have spent 5 'd/had picked up
6 have listened 7 have said 8 hadn't wasted

5B

1
1 e 2 b 3 a 4 f 5 g 6 d 7 h 8 c
2
1 broke into 2 planned 3 evade arrest
4 leaving the scene of the crime
5 charge him with 6 plead guilty
7 sentenced to
3
1 are 2 is 3 person 4 times 5 were
6 much 7 keys 8 lend
4
1 several times 2 Correct 3 Correct
4 a little time 5 No person 6 Correct
7 There is 8 None of the six children
5
1 few 2 every 3 all 4 None 5 several
6 a few 7 Both 8 Neither

5C

1
1 interest 2 recession 3 investments
4 savings 5 pension 6 income 7 bargain
8 donation 9 inflation 10 budget
2
1 interest 2 savings 3 pension/income
4 recession 5 inflation 6 pension/income
7 donation 8 budget 9 bargains
10 investment
3
1 qualified 2 dangerous 3 wrong 4 good
5 disappointed 6 easy
4
1 perfectly safe 2 completely different
3 absolutely ridiculous 4 bitterly cold
5 widely available 6 relatively simple
5
1 c 2 d 3 d 4 c 5 c 6 c

5D

1
1 mark 2 alone 3 on 4 mess
5 message 6 home 7 around 8 me
2
1 d 2 a 3 b 4 c
3
1 It's no big deal. (b)
2 I had nothing to do with it. (c)
3 I'll sort it out, I promise. (a)
4 Try not to do it again. (b)
5 It's got nothing to do with me. (c)
6 I should have been more careful. (a)
7 Well, who did then? (d)
8 I'm so sorry, did I spill your drink? (a)
4
1 own 2 deal 3 sort 4 fault 5 blame
6 then
5
1 Let's try to find a solution.
2 What about if Andy and I
3 I don't think that's going to work
4 I understand (that)
5 Why don't I see if I
6 That sounds reasonable
7 It makes sense because

Reading

1
The cost of items
2
1 e 2 c 3 a 4 f 5 d 6 b

3
1 50 percent 2 Nothing 3 The price per item
4 (Calculate and) compare prices
5 You get more 6 Remember prices (of items)
7 It hasn't changed 8 Evaluate a deal
4
1 push up 2 evaluate 3 multi-pack
4 a good deal 5 labelled 6 economical
7 trick 8 forced 9 bulk-buy
10 hard-earned
5
1 truly 2 close 3 fell 4 top 5 much
6
2, 3, 4

Listening

1
b
2
1 time 2 abroad 3 thefts 4 failed
5 bank accounts 6 technical 7 Hackers
8 payment system 9 behind
3
1 b 2 d 3 a 4 e 5 c

Writing

1
b
2
1 short, dark, straight, wavy, receding
2 symmetrical 3 deep brown 4 elegant
5 full 6 above average height, slim, broad
7 deep, soft 8 shy, confident
3
bald: hair   freckles: face   high-pitched: voice
muscular: body   prominent: nose   stubble: face
thick: hair   thin: hair, nose, mouth, body
wide: eyes, mouth
4
… dark as the night sky   … as deep as the ocean
… rich and soft like velvet   … as strong as an ox
5
1 c 2 g 3 a 4 e 5 b 6 h 7 f 8 d
6–8
Students' own answers.

UNIT 6

6A

1
be a pain, be out of this world, be over the moon,
be a piece of cake, cost an arm and a leg,
drive me up the wall, take my breath away
2
1 world 2 breath 3 leg 4 wall 5 cake
6 cover 7 moon 8 a pain
3
1 takes my breath away 2 drives me up the wall
3 judge a book by its cover
4 cost an arm and a leg 5 over the moon
6 a pain 7 a piece of cake 8 out of this world
4
1 going 2 to go 3 living 4 to get
5 telling 6 to buy 7 locking 8 Having
5
1 We considered getting a dog last year.
2 It isn't/'s not worth crying over a broken dish.
3 It's easy to get around the city on foot.
4 Megan keeps sending me really funny gifs.
5 Do you remember meeting me for the first time?
6 I can't wait to have a lovely, relaxing bath tonight.
7 It was good of you to come round and help
  yesterday.
8 Dom messaged me this morning to invite me
  for dinner.
6
1 watching 2 laughing 3 eating/having
4 having 5 to have 6 Playing 7 having
8 complaining/moaning 9 moaning/complaining

6B

1
1 fell out 2 conflict 3 stay calm 4 bond
5 tension 6 build trust 7 interrupting
8 praise
2
1 c 2 a 3 b 4 a 5 b 6 a 7 c
3
1 'd been living 2 he'd meet 3 wanted
4 could go 5 where the match was
6 to be quiet
4
1 had moved 2 'd/had got
3 involves/involved 4 'd/had been feeling
5 not to 6 knew 7 were
8 misses/missed

6C

1
1 reminding 2 threatened 3 denied
4 insisted 5 refuses 6 convinced
7 apologised 8 blames
2
1 accused 2 deny 3 insist 4 convince
5 refused 6 threatened 7 advised
8 blamed 9 reminded 10 agreed
11 apologise 12 admitted
3
1 breaking 2 to let 3 playing 4 to pay
5 to increase 6 on taking 7 us to get
8 to give
4
1 d Norah insisted on paying it
2 f She accused me of borrowing her clothes
3 c I've agreed to help a friend move house
4 b I admit having one or two
5 e Remind me never to ask you for advice
6 a David's threatened to cancel the party

Listening

1
a
2
1 Podcast 2 2 Podcast 1 3 Podcast 1
4 Podcast 2 5 Podcast 2 6 Podcast 1
7 Both 8 Podcast 2 9 Both 10 Podcast 1
3
1 asked for 2 profits 3 job satisfaction
4 calm, friendly 5 disappointing 6 listening
4
1 b 2 a 3 a 4 a 5 b 6 a
5
1 d 2 e 3 b 4 f 5 a 6 c
6
1 Podcast 2 2 Both 3 Podcast 1

Reading

1
c
2
1 h 2 p 3 k, l 4 n 5 g 6 c 7 n, o
8 a, m
3
1 T
2 F *He also likes falling asleep in front of the TV.*
3 F *He knows he shouldn't do it.*
4 T
5 F *He feels it's a depressing habit.*
6 F *He says that he's heard this is the case, not
   that he does it.*
7 T
8 F *They remind her of her own childhood.*
4
1 a 2 b 3 b 4 a 5 a 6 a

5
1 catch sight of   2 proving you wrong
3 break the habit   4 chill out
5 stuffed my face
6 keep our feet on the ground

Writing

1
1 hotel, refund
2 electric toothbrush, replacement product
2
1 a, d   2 b, e   3 f   4 c, g
3
1 I am making a claim for a full refund.
 (purpose 2)
2 I hope to hear from you at your earliest
 convenience. (purpose 4)
3 Please accept this email as a claim for a refund.
 (purpose 4)
4 I am writing to complain about your event.
 (purpose 1)
5 This product is not fit for purpose. (purpose 3)
6 I believe the product is still under warranty.
 (purpose 3)
4
1 hopefully   2 clearly, obviously   3 frankly
4 unfortunately
5
Hope/luck/unhappiness: luckily, sadly
Surprise: astonishingly, naturally, predictably
Other: reluctantly
6
1 Sadly   2 Predictably   3 Naturally
4 Luckily   5 reluctantly   6 Astonishingly
7–10
Students' own answers.

UNIT 7

7A

1
1 standard/living   2 Unemployment
3 Homelessness   4 social unrest
2
1 inequality   2 life expectancy
3 living standards   4 energy efficiency
5 inequality   6 energy efficiency
7 healthcare   8 poverty   9 life expectancy
3
1 f   2 d   3 b   4 a   5 e   6 c
4
1 long   2 soon   3 when   4 unless   5 If
6 provided
5
1 Unless you get the large size, the shirt won't
 fit me.
2 When my dog sees me, she comes running
 every time!
3 I won't come with you if you don't want me to.
4 You'll do fine in the exams as long as you
 revise.
5 Provided that Jack does his part of the report
 soon, we'll finish it by 3 p.m.
6 My car always stops working when I need it
 the most.

7B

1
1 e   2 d   3 b   4 a   5 c
2
1 will   2 definitely   3 doubt   4 are
5 won't   6 possible   7 won't   8 unlikely
3
1 e   2 b   3 d   4 h   5 g   6 a   7 c   8 f

4
1 shot   2 place   3 sense   4 profit   5 job
6 without   7 a hand   8 risk
5
1 taking a risk   2 make a profit
3 give it your best shot
4 doing a lot of research
5 getting a good deal   6 Give priority
7 do without   8 Take charge

7C

1
Across: 7 sister-in-law   8 client
9 brother-in-law
Down: 1 ex-partner   2 senior colleague
3 acquaintance   4 classmate   5 co-worker
6 flatmate
2
1 acquaintance   2 co-workers   3 flatmate
4 clients   5 ex-partner   6 brother-in-law
7 sister-in-law   8 classmates
3
1 It seems to me that Lyn and Ellie have fallen out.
2 It feels as if it's going to rain.
3 It strikes me that we're spending a lot of
 money.
4 It sounds as though you're having a hard time.
5 It occurs to me that I've never been here
 before.
6 It looks as if you've had a great day.
4
1 a, b   2 c   3 a   4 c   5 b   6 a
5
1 that/as if/as though you're not very happy
2 to me that the shops close early on a Sunday
3 out that I didn't have any battery
4 me that anyone eats this awful fast food
5 as if/though this is a lovely house
6 worries/concerns me that Tammy always
 looks fed up

7D

1
1 agenda   2 item   3 topic   4 business
5 talk   6 gone   7 move   8 through
9 input   10 come
2
1 Let's get down to business.
2 Has everyone met Gill from Accounts?
3 The next item on the agenda is our budget.
4 Our goal today is to decide on a new project.
5 Let's make a start, shall we?
6 I think you all know Eduardo.
7 It's good to see you all here.
8 The purpose of this meeting is to share new
 ideas.
3
a copy of the agenda not *diary*
let's get started/let's begin not *begun*
The purpose of today's meeting not *role*
item on the agenda not *object*
4
1 have to stop you there
2 what are your thoughts   3 've gone off topic
4 maybe you could tell   5 Let's move on to
6 to hear your views
5
1 b   2 f   3 a   4 d   5 e   6 c

Reading

1
1 c   2 d   3 a   4 b
2
1 Writer 2   2 Writer 3   3 Writer 3   4 Writer 4
5 Writer 1   6 Writer 4   7 Writer 2   8 Writer 4
9 Writer 3   10 Writer 1   11 Writer 2
12 Writer 1

3
1 fast transfer   2 bathroom mirror
3 on our way   4 psychological
5 hack our bodies
4
1 b   2 f   3 d   4 h   5 a   6 e   7 c   8 g
5
1 suffers from   2 analysed my saliva
3 monitor our health   4 cure all major illnesses
5 absorb that emotion
6 overcome physical difficulties
7 potential problem   8 receive treatment

Listening

1
1 retire   2 (full-time) job   3 15/fifteen
4 day trips/staycations   5 children
2
1 home   2 loans   3 10–15   4 meals
5 holidays   6 meals   7 camping   8 interest
9 income   10 goals
3
Comment 2

Writing

1
May not *March*
75 people not *65*
Mark's cousin to DJ not *brother*
Lisa to get paperwork from *the police* not *the
council*
Discuss £ of tickets, not *DJ* next week
2
1 T   2 T   3 F   4 T   5 F   6 T
3
About/regarding: re.   And/plus: +
Approximately: approx.   Compared with: c.f.
Increase: ↑   Necessary: nec.   People: ppl
Price/cost: £   Through: thru   Week: wk
Weekend: w/e
4
Because = b/c   Decrease = ↓   Especially = esp.
Information = info.   Number = no.   Very = v.
With = w/   Without = w/o
5
Suggested answers:
1 Demand for products this month > last month
2 Sales this year low c.f. last year
3 Sales ↓ x 30%
4 No other sales information b/c Maria off sick
5 Need to do more to advertise in local
 newspapers, online etc.
6 Need a meeting w/ Tom re. our new product.
7 Promotion of product v. imp.
8 NB. Tom's on holiday next wk.
6
Suggested answers:
1 Need to get a plumber out to fix taps in toilets
 on 1st, 2nd etc. floor.
2 ↑ no. of invitations to approx. 30.
3 Need to do research to get more info. re. the
 area.
4 Ken will hire mini bus. Everyone else go w/ him.
5 Recent storm → power cut in 3 villages
6 Dan to call Sally re DJ. She can book someone if
 nec.
7
Possible answer:
Things to do before our holiday
1 Research cheaper car park. Last year's £↑ x
 50%.
2 Speak to Ed re. plants, cat etc. Buy gift from
 Spain.
3 Buy new suitcase online w/ four wheels.
4 Get 1 x small bottle sun cream at w/e. Buy
 more during wk at hotel shop.
5 Check travel insurance. Get more if nec.
6 Put passports in case.
7 Download music, films, books etc. onto phones.
 Take games e.g. cards.
8 Order 500 euros online. Pick up in town. Use
 debit cards.

8A

1
1 trick 2 survive 3 capture 4 rescue
5 confront 6 overcome
2
1 murdered 2 goes on a mission 3 capture
4 betrays 5 tricked 6 rescues 7 survives
8 face
3
1 d 2 g 3 a 4 c 5 h 6 e 7 f 8 b
4
1 a 2 a,c 3 c 4 b 5 b,c 6 b
5
1 you were in a film, what would it/the film be/
  what film would it be?
2 I'd be
3 could do/would be able to do if I had
4 if I had the chance
5 would be
6 I'd make
7 'd/would be
8 I had
9 I'd be
10 'd fight
11 If I could have
12 it'd be

8B

1
1 spotted 2 traced 3 disguise 4 pursuing
5 head for 6 identify 7 deceived
8 tracking
2
1 b 2 a 3 c 4 a 5 b 6 a 7 c
3
1 If I hadn't gone to university, I wouldn't be a
  teacher.
2 We might not have met if I'd decided not to go
  to that party.
3 I'd feel OK right now if I hadn't eaten so much
  food.
4 If I'd seen you, I would have come and said
  hello.
5 We wouldn't have run out of petrol if you'd
  filled the car up.
6 I'd still be sitting in my car right now if you
  hadn't warned me about the traffic.
7 If we'd got here earlier, we may have got a
  better seat.
8 You might not have come if I'd told you Harry
  would be here.
4
1 'd have lost; hadn't heard
2 'd listened; wouldn't have misunderstood
3 'd feel; 'd had
4 wouldn't be; hadn't sat
5 might not have hit; 'd left
6 would have been; 'd taken
7 'd studied; might/would have been
8 'd messaged; wouldn't have had to

8C

1
abstract artwork, landscape, oil painting,
original artwork, still life, water colour
2
1 oil painting 2 collage 3 artwork
4 an original artwork 5 landscape 6 statues
7 portrait 8 installation
3
1 portrait 2 watercolour 3 statue
4 installation 5 still life 6 sketch 7 print
8 abstract artwork
4
1 a 2 a 3 a 4 b 5 b

5
1 Despite the fact that the museum is in need of
  repair, it's a gorgeous building.
2 I want to like still life. However, I find it boring.
3 Although fake paintings aren't original, they're
  still art.
4 I can't do simple drawings in spite of it being
  easy for many people.
5 Watercolours don't appeal to me even though
  they are very popular.
6
1 f 2 c 3 d 4 a 5 e 6 b

Listening

1
Sofia
2
1 b 2 a 3 b 4 a 5 c 6 c
3
1 stick man 2 works of art 3 humanity
4 miserable 5 gallery 6 building owners
7 security people
8 work together/compromise
4
1 g 2 c 3 e 4 b 5 a 6 d 7 h 8 f
5
1 S 2 L 3 L 4 S

Reading

1
1 d 2 b 3 f 4 c 5 a 6 e
2
1 b 2 a 3 a 4 c 5 c 6 b
3
1 a balancing act 2 maintain
3 associated with 4 alarmed by
5 (be) aware of 6 truly
7 (do something) to your heart's content
8 spoiler
4
1 alarmed by 2 aware of 3 heart's content
4 truly 5 associated with 6 maintain
7 spoiler 8 balancing act
5
1 search engine 2 delete 3 changing
4 digital footprint 5 security questions
6 feature

Writing

1
+: focus on characters, the script, the humour
−: the length of the film
B: the storyline, the action scenes
2
1 b 2 d 3 a 4 a 5 c
3
It doesn't say what is not good about the book or
make a recommendation.
4
1 c 2 e 3 d 4 b 5 a
5
1 played 2 little-known 3 by 4 illustrates
5 stars 6 plot 7 character 8 explores
6
1 Film 2 Book 3 Film 4 Both 5 Film
6 Both 7 Both 8 Both
7–9
Students' own answers.

9A

1
1 hoax 2 Motive 3 account for 4 turns out
5 remains 6 evidence 7 clues 8 identify
2
1 red herring 2 evidence 3 hoax 4 victim
5 clue 6 motive
3
1 c 2 e 3 b 4 a 5 d
4
1 must have turned 2 can't have gone
3 been getting 4 must have seen 5 Correct
6 must have noticed
5
1 must have been 2 might have been
3 can't have bought 4 might have had
5 might also have been 6 must have consisted

9B

1
1 c 2 b 3 a 4 c 5 a 6 b 7 c 8 b
2
1 suspect 2 misunderstood 3 knowledge
4 fake 5 conclusion 6 theories
7 assumption 8 observations
3
1 wearing 2 to give 3 to see 4 do
5 playing 6 to come 7 to ride 8 move
4
1 to turn 2 was 3 to do 4 to come
5 leaving 6 'll pick 7 haven't paid/didn't pay
8 to pay 9 to go 10 trying 11 to fix
12 speak
5
1 I can't imagine anyone enjoying this music.
2 Susie wants to make dinner for us.
3 I've just realised (that) we've met before.
4 My boss has recommended (that) I apply for a
  promotion.
5 My parents made me go to bed really early
  when I was young.
6 Dan's asked me to go to a wedding with him
  but I can't go.
7 I assure you that this is our lowest possible
  price.
8 Sophie's just agreed to let me cut her hair.

9C

1
1 d 2 h 3 a 4 g 5 e 6 c 7 b 8 f
2
1 make out 2 stands out 3 comes across
4 stick it out 5 turned out OK 6 get over
7 let her family down 8 figure out
3
1 B 2 A 3 A 4 B 5 A 6 B 7 B 8 A
4
1 Who came up with that silly plan?
2 Mike's still getting over the flu.
3 I need to stop worrying and get on with my life.
4 My parents make up different stories about
  how they met.
5 Your orange car certainly stands out from the
  rest!
6 Let's think through the possible consequences
  carefully.
5
1 let my family down/let down my family
2 made out
3 made up an excuse/made an excuse up
4 get over my disappointment
5 get on with my life
6 stood out
7 turned/turning out well

1
1 wrong 2 stock 3 down 4 arrive
5 expected 6 lost 7 booked 8 refused

2
1 e 2 b 3 g 4 i 5 d 6 a 7 h 8 f
9 c

3
1 Can you put me through to reception, please?
2 What is it concerning?
3 I'm calling about a job application.
4 I'll put you through to Marcus.
5 Stefania will be able to answer your questions.
6 Is there someone there who could help me?
7 Could you call back in a few minutes?

4
1 The problem is 2 Would it be possible
3 try and come 4 got a problem
5 Let me check 6 refund the money
7 calling about 8 'd like you 9 get a call back

5
1 It's about my car / I'm calling about my car
2 I'd like you to take a look at it
3 I'll have a word with my/the manager
4 there must be a mistake
5 Let me check to see what happened
6 I want to know why that is

Reading

1
1 d 2 a 3 c 4 e 5 b

2
1 T 2 F 3 F 4 T 5 F 6 T 7 F 8 T
9 F 10 T 11 F 12 T

3
1 c 2 a 3 b

4
1 poor relations with 2 launch a manhunt
3 publicity 4 claimed 5 remote
6 satisfy our curiosity 7 enabled us
8 an ideal world

5
1 publicity 2 claim 3 launch a manhunt
4 satisfy 5 enabled 6 remote

Listening

1
a

2
1 c 2 a 3 a 4 b 5 b

Writing

1
c

2
1 c 2 a 3 a 4 a 5 b

3
2 c 3 a 4 b

4
1 There is plenty of evidence that ...
2 In addition to that ...
3 In summary, ...
4 I am convinced that ...
5 To summarise, ...
6 This is conclusive proof that ...
7 I strongly believe that ...
8 The main reason is that ...

5
I: 4, 7 M: 1, 2, 6, 8 C: 3, 5

6–8
Students' own answers.

UNIT 10

10A

1
1 my true vocation 2 My great passion
3 like-minded friends 4 artistic ability
5 unique talent 6 sense of adventure
7 a place of my own 8 my soul mate
9 place I can call home

2
1 core 2 life 3 vocation 4 sense 5 soul
6 home 7 adventure 8 unique

3
1 b 2 d 3 c 4 f 5 g 6 h 7 e 8 a

4
1 be seeing 2 we'll still be waiting
3 I'll have finished 4 Correct 5 have left
6 will be living

5
1 'll still be working 2 'll have got
3 Will you be going 4 'll be passing
5 'll have finished 6 'll have read
7 Will you still be working
8 'll probably have finished 9 won't be living
10 'll have moved

10B

1
1 big break 2 unknown
3 taken the world by storm 4 an instant hit
5 started out 6 legacy
7 being in the public eye

2
1 b 2 d 3 a 4 c 5 f 6 e

3
1 c 2 a 3 b 4 a 5 c 6 a 7 b 8 c

4
1 dogs 2 the plates 3 ~~the~~ Chicago
4 the police station 5 the most amazing thing
6 ~~The~~ Inner beauty is 7 the Sahara Desert
8 The one with the black cap

5
1 The Dutch bred orange carrots
2 the British town of Dull (was) linked with the American town of Boring
3 the spaceship which landed on the moon
4 a person gets rid of about 35 kg of skin
5 threw a party for time travellers
6 didn't send the invitations
7 turned up to the party
8 the Middle Ages in Europe
9 a moment was equal to 90 seconds
10 an hour was divided into 40 moments

10C

1
densely populated, good-looking, five-year, hard-up, high-tech, middle-aged, part-time, self-confident, strong-willed, well-educated

2
1 short 2 known 3 minute 4 built
5 behaved 6 narrow 7 run 8 centred

3
1 brightly-lit 2 broken-down 3 well-off
4 absent-minded 5 state-of-the-art
6 internet-connected 7 well-known
8 part-time 9 15-year 10 so-called

4
1 enforce 2 install 3 fined 4 introduce
5 put up 6 charge 7 educated
8 discourage

5
1 c 2 a 3 c 4 b 5 a 6 b 7 b 8 c

Listening

1
They're all fiction

2
1 All of it 2 Something bad 3 (Around) 100
4 Silly 5 The Equator 6 The shape
7 (Survival) tricks 8 A handle

3
1 sentence 2 seven/7 times
3 maximum speed 4 tricks 5 the same time
6 forgetful

4
1 T 2 T 3 F 4 T 5 F 6 F

5
1 c 2 b 3 e 4 f 5 a 6 d

Reading

1
c

2
1 b 2 d 3 e 4 f 5 a 6 c

3
1 F 2 T 3 F 4 T 5 T 6 F 7 T
8 F

4
1, 3, 5, 6

5
1 a 2 b 3 a 4 b 5 a

6
1 speed by 2 overall 3 rush
4 not a bed of roses 5 perspective
6 settle down 7 made the most of 8 loyal

7
1 settle down 2 a bed of roses 3 rush
4 perspective 5 make the most 6 loyal
7 overall 8 sped by

Writing

1
1 a 2 e 3 b 4 f 5 d 6 c

2
1 F 2 F 3 T 4 T 5 T 6 T

3
1 b 2 a 3 c 4 c 5 a

4
1 help 2 afraid 3 Find 4 time zones
5 far better 6 long way 7 look like
8 feel the need

5–7
Students' own answers.